Angela Diller

THE
SPLENDOR OF MUSIC

by

ANGELA DILLER

G. SCHIRMER, Inc.
New York

For
Kate Stearns Page
Her Book

CONTENTS

v

ACKNOWLEDGMENTS

The author wishes to acknowledge an Award of the John Simon Guggenheim Memorial Foundation, which has contributed in securing leisure time for the writing of this book.

Among the many friends who have been helpful through the stimulating exchange of ideas, my special thanks go to Henry and Sophie Drinker, and to March Cost.

Ruth Stoneridge has given invaluable assistance in preparing the manuscript. She has twice followed it from New England to California and back to New England. For her editorial help my hearty thanks, with much affection.

To Kate Stearns Page, without whose deep interest and continuing faith this book could not have been completed, my love and gratitude.

Long Pond, Plymouth
Massachusetts

FOREWORD

> . . . and to know
> Rather consists in opening out a way
> Whence the imprisoned splendor may escape,
> Than in effecting entry for a light
> Supposed to be without. . . .

From *Paracelsus*

By Robert Browning

This book concerns itself with two "imprisoned splendors." The first is the splendor of Music that lies behind the symbols on printed pages. This music has a life of its own and is waiting to be released by us, as we translate these symbols into sounds.

The other imprisoned splendor is the innate capacity for understanding and creating music that resides in almost every human soul. This capacity is waiting to be released and developed.

The fusing of these two splendors is one of the important aims of music education.

After more than fifty years of music teaching, I am increasingly aware of the variety and richness of this stimulating and rewarding profession. I have written this book with the hope that it may be of service to other teachers, as well as to students and the general reader, through the discussion of some of our common problems.

Part I. The Interpreter

The "imprisoned splendor" locked behind the notes on the printed pages of music can only be brought into the world of sound, and thus communicated to the hearer, through the Performer, whom we call the Interpreter. He is the necessary intermediary between the composer and the listener.

How different is our contact with the work of a painter or a sculptor from our contact with the work of a composer! We can view a painting by Vermeer or a statue by Donatello, and without the need of an intermediary we see the creation as it was completed by the artist. But how can we get in touch with a Brahms symphony unless we have interpreters?

A symphony exists first as idea and as sound in the mind and heart of the composer. He writes the symbols of these sounds on paper. But the score of his symphony may lie untouched on a shelf for years. The music, like the Sleeping Beauty, or like Brünnhilde on her rock, waits silently for its awakening. The great responsibility of bringing this music into the world of sound rests on interpreters.

A trained musician, on reading a page of printed or written music, can hear something of what it sounds like in his mind's ear. But for almost everyone, music requires re-creation by a singer or an instrumentalist or a chorus or an orchestra. Thus we might say that People are Music's Necessity.

What a wonderful treasury of music has come down to us through the years as it has been interpreted and re-interpreted! Music, the most evanescent of the arts, never dies. A great musical composition can achieve newness of life through a great interpretation, years after the composer has laid down his pen. The Eroica Symphony has a rebirth every time it is performed, and the St. Matthew Passion a resurrection whenever it is sung.

But because interpreters were lacking, much music has been written that the composers themselves never heard performed. For example, what a loss it would be if Schubert's great C major Symphony were

1

not part of our musical heritage! Yet this vortex of musical energy and beauty was unknown until Schumann saw the score, realized its overpowering significance, and planned at once for its performance. On a visit to Vienna ten years after Schubert's death, Schumann found the unpublished manuscript of this symphony "buried in dust and darkness." He writes with warmth and delight of this marvelous music, and tells most movingly the story of its discovery in an article for the *Neue Zeitschrift für Musik.* He describes the work in detail, and speaks of "the glow of romanticism that everywhere accompanies Franz Schubert," and of the symphony's "heavenly length." He sent the score to his friend Mendelssohn, who as soon as possible performed it in Leipzig with the Gewandhaus Orchestra. Of this first performance Schumann writes:

> The symphony produced such an effect among us as none has produced since Beethoven's. Artists and connoisseurs united in its praise, and I heard a few words spoken by Mendelssohn, who had studied it with the utmost care for its perfect success, that I should have been only too happy, had such a thing been possible, to report to the living Schubert as the gladdest of glad tidings. . . . There is no danger that this work will ever be overlooked or forgotten. It bears within itself everlasting youth.

Since this historic first performance, how many hundreds of times have interpreters had the high privilege of re-creating this great music, and how many thousands of listeners have thrilled to this noble expression of Schubert's genius!

A great piece of music, like a great play, carries within itself many meanings and the possibility of many valid interpretations.

Beethoven's Ninth Symphony, for example, as conducted by Toscanini, Walter, Weingartner, or Karajan, comes to us in four quite different interpretations. Each conductor is dedicated to the unfolding of Beethoven's ideas. And yet each views the composition through his own temperament and against his own musical background.

But who is to say which reading Beethoven would have regarded as fufilling most completely his own intentions? And did Beethoven himself have an unwavering conception of his own work, or did he perhaps have different ideas about its interpretation at different times or in different moods? It is even possible that "he builded better than he knew," and might have heard in any one of these interpretations certain aspects of the music that he did not realize he had written.

The mystery of the opening measures leading to the tumultuous descent of the D minor chord, the relentless rhythm of the Scherzo, the curving melody of the slow movement, the astonishing development in the last movement, where we first hear the theme coming from the depths of the orchestra, sung by the 'cellos and double basses, and rising higher and higher, culminating in voices singing triumphantly Schiller's "Ode to Joy"— all these are waiting to be released again and again by new interpreters.

We, as listeners, have all had the experience of hearing a new interpretation of a familiar piece, when it has been revealed to us in such a new light that we have exclaimed, "I feel that I have never heard this piece before!" This experience keeps us from being dogmatic, and from thinking that the one interpretation with which we are familiar is the only possible one. Perhaps there are as many valid interpretations of a great composition as there are dedicated and inspired interpreters of the work at any given time. Perhaps the work itself is the sum total— and more— of all these possible interpretations!

We may not agree with a thoughtful and sincere interpretation of a piece of music, yet we can listen receptively to it. But we must disagree if the music is given only a superficial, dull-eared reading, or if the interpreter regards the composition primarily as a vehicle for his own self-expression.

Recently I heard a brilliant but saddening performance of the Schumann Piano Concerto. The young virtuoso who was playing the solo part had a conception of the last movement that was quite different from anything indicated in the score. He began the recapitulation at the original tempo, but from then on he played the rest of the movement with a steady accelerando and crescendo that ignored completely the delicate dynamic details that Schumann had indicated. It was as though Caesar's legions were trampling over a flower garden. The effect was tremendously exciting, and the audience burst into thunderous applause. But I wanted to weep, as I heard what was happening to the Concerto and to Schumann. Here was a gifted young man who was so involved in expressing his own ego that he entirely lost sight of the fact that he was interpreting something someone else had written. He had overlaid the composer's intentions with his own idea of what the music should mean. This performance could only have been called "Mis-Interpretation."

One's own conception of a composition is not a static affair. The greater the music, the more there is for us to discover. Every musician knows this to be true, and it should be true of all of us. The more we learn of all music, the more we have to bring to any piece that we are studying. So, with the years, our interpretation of a composition necessarily changes. It may be that we have a new understanding of a melodic line, or we suddenly comprehend the significance of a harmonic progression, or we discover a relationship between certain passages of which we had not been aware before. Today's interpretation of a composition represents our present knowledge of it. As the days go by, we hope to discover more and more of its meaning.

So we see the interpretation of a piece of music is the process of bringing to light something that already exists. This is as true of a child learning to play a folk tune as it is of an adult exploring the Goldberg Variations.

Of course, with each of us, there is some music that we will understand instinctively, just as there are some people to whom we are drawn and whom we understand at once. There *is* such a thing as love at first sight! Other music we will have to study longer in order to interpret, just as other people are more difficult to know. The greater the breadth of our musical interest, the wider the scope of music we can interpret.

In performing great music, we identify ourselves with it. With part of our mind we are aware of what we are doing, but we are also aware of what the music itself is doing. We should have studied it so well that while we play we are re-creating it. It is a combination of objective and subjective experience.

On the Interpreter, whether he be artist or teacher or student, rests the responsibility of re-creating music. He does this for the sake of the music, for the sake of the composer, for his own sake, and for the sake of the listeners who, through him, enter this world of sound.

Part II. The Teacher
INTRODUCTION

The profession of piano teaching is infinitely varied, dealing as it does with people and with music. The teacher comes in contact with all sorts and conditions of people: young and old, gifted and not gifted, quick and slow, facile and clumsy, imaginative and literal-minded. The teacher has the privilege of putting all of these diverse people into touch with all sorts and conditions of music: new and old, serious and gay, simple and complex, juvenile and sophisticated. The teacher's job is to bring people and music together.

The teacher will have an exciting experience when she* helps an older pupil to understand and play beautifully a great composition, such as the Schumann Fantasia, or a Chopin scherzo, or perhaps a Prokofiev sonata. But there is also musical pleasure in helping a little child to understand and play beautifully a simple folk tune, or a Mozart minuet, or one of the Bartók pieces for children.

The size of a work of art is not the measure of its greatness. A small work of art can be a great work of art. Dürer's famous drawing, "Praying Hands," measuring slightly over 7 inches by 11, is a great work of art. So also is Tintoretto's "Paradiso"—the largest painting in the world, covering 2,856 square feet in the Ducal Palace in Venice. Wordsworth's sonnet beginning "Nuns fret not at their convent's narrow walls," is a complete work of art within "its scanty plot of ground," bounded by 14 lines. So also is Shakespeare's play, "Othello," which is told in 5 acts and 15 scenes, and takes 3 hours to unfold.

So it is with music. Schubert wrote a perfect song, "An die Musik," in 23 measures—it takes less than 3 minutes to sing both stanzas. And he also wrote the C major Symphony "of heavenly length," which lasts nearly an hour. Both of these compositions are great music.

---

* At the present time, in this country, more women than men are engaged in music teaching. Therefore, in this Part, the teacher is referred to as *she*. This does not imply any superiority of she's over he's, but merely recognizes that in point of numbers, the she's have it.

Little pieces and large pieces, children and adults, all are within the circle of the experienced teacher's sympathetic understanding.

The teacher will have a more interesting life if she is dealing with many kinds of students who are playing many kinds of music. This variety will help to keep the teacher herself musically alive. For example, in teaching a Mozart minuet to a small child, her perspective will be broader if she has been working with an older student on the Schumann Fantasia than if she taught nothing but children's pieces. It is the breadth of the teacher's own musical experience on which she will draw continuously to illumine all of her teaching.

An advertisement that I read many years ago expresses this idea. John Wanamaker was extolling the virtues of a new stock of blankets: they were very warm and light, they came in beautiful colors, the texture and durability were excellent, and they were moderately priced. But their greatest virtue was their unusual width. The line that announced this in the advertisement was "It's the part that hangs over that keeps you warm!"

Similarly, it is the breadth of the teacher's musical interest that keeps her teaching warm and vital.

WHY CHOOSE THE PIANO?

The following are some of the reasons for choosing the piano as an instrument on which to study music:

1) Because a beginner can make music on the piano more easily and completely than on any other instrument. The piano, with its wide compass and its pedals, makes it possible for a young student from the beginning to experience Harmony, as well as the other two elements of musical composition, Rhythm and Melody.

2) Because, from its very nature, it is the easiest instrument on which a beginner can learn some of the fundamentals of theory — for example, the patterns of chord and scale formation.

3) Because the piano is an ideal instrument on which to investigate the language of music, that is, to play by ear and to improvise.

4) Because if the piano is in good condition, the music will be played in tune (which cannot always be said of the young string player's first efforts at music-making!).

5) Because, although it is primarily a solo instrument, it is also an ensemble instrument, and much wonderful music has been written for the piano in combination with other instruments.

6) Because it is the most useful instrument for family music and for social gatherings of all kinds. Despite the advent of records, radio, and television, a piano is to be found in most homes.

7) Because it is possible to become acquainted with much music in addition to that written for piano solo. Many arrangements of orchestral, chamber, and vocal music have been made for piano solo and for piano duet.

8) Most important of all, because a wealth of great musical literature has been written for the piano, waiting to be brought to life by those who understand it and have learned to read and play it.

Exception: Sometimes a musical child is so unpianistic that he should start instrumental work on a string or wind instrument rather than on the piano to which he is obviously allergic.

I remember one seven-year-old boy whose musical education began with class work in musicianship, and piano lessons. He was very musical, had a fine ear, a good voice, and an uncanny sense of phrasing. He had delicate, agile fingers, but was acutely unhappy when he tried to make music with them on the keyboard. After a few lessons, his wise teacher suggested that he continue with the class work, but drop the piano lessons, and start playing the recorder and then the flute. His light, tapering fingers were at home at once on the flute, which eventually he played as an artist.

Better to be a happy flutist than a clumsy and unhappy pianist!

QUALIFICATIONS OF A
PIANO TEACHER

The piano teacher's task is four-fold:
1) To teach her students the language of music;
2) To help them to study compositions written in this language;
3) To teach them how to play these compositions on the piano;
4) To give them a wide interest in all kinds of music. Paraphrasing Bacon, to help them to realize that the entire field of music is their realm.

A certain degree of pianistic skill and a knowledge of piano literature are, of course, requisite for anyone who is going to teach the piano. Obviously, the broader her experience of music in many fields, the more the teacher will have to bring to every piano lesson. But aside from her special training, there are temperamental qualities that are desirable in anyone who teaches music.

On one occasion I asked a group of teachers to write a list of what they considered the most important qualifications of a piano teacher. I was surprised to find, on reading over the papers, that more than half of the group listed "patience" as the most important. We talked the matter over at some length, and finally agreed that perhaps with a dull, slow child, patience was a virtue. But surely the qualifications that should come at the head of the list are the teacher's enthusiasm for music, and the desire and ability to awaken this enthusiasm in others — the ability to stimulate the pupil's interest and curiosity. We teachers must have a never-ceasing interest and delight in music itself, and realize that one of the great joys in teaching is to kindle a fire in another's mind. A liking for people and an ability to get along congenially with them are, of course, essential.

Obviously, if music teaching is only a financial stop-gap, it should never be undertaken. A girl who plays fairly well may want to "take a few pupils" to earn some money between leaving school and getting married. If this is her only reason for giving piano lessons, she should do practically anything to earn money, except teach music!

LEARNING HOW TO TEACH

(Suggestions for the Piano Student
Who Wishes to Become a Teacher)

In many parts of the country it is possible for a student who wishes to be a piano teacher to attend teacher-training courses. In one school with which I have been connected, a comprehensive and closely integrated course is given over a two-year period: the student studies piano playing, ear training, harmony, counterpoint, and analysis; she attends classes in piano pedagogy, in materials and methods, and in keyboard improvisation; she observes lessons given by experienced teachers; and, supervised by members of the faculty, she does practice-teaching herself. With this background, the young student is fairly well prepared to start teaching on her own responsibility.

In many communities, however, no teacher-training courses are available. Yet every young piano teacher needs help in learning how to teach. It is not enough to love music and love people in order to be a music teacher. A young doctor serves a long internship when his work with his patients is supervised, and only after several years of this training does he go out into the world as a full-fledged practitioner. Young music teachers also need much supervised experience before they start off on their own.

Unfortunately, however, all over the country, anyone who wants to teach piano can do so without let or hindrance. I have often felt that perhaps an inexperienced teacher should pay the pupils on whom she experiments in the process of discovering whether she can or cannot teach.

If you cannot attend teacher-training courses, your own piano teacher would perhaps be willing to have you serve as a sort of musical apprentice to her, by supervising the practicing of some of her young pupils. You can attend the pupil's lesson, observing experienced teaching, and the teacher will tell you what is to be stressed in the child's practice period. Since a young pupil's early lessons will be largely confined to learning how to work at home, it is helpful at the beginning for the child to have aid in organizing his time productively when

10

he practices. (However, the child should have one or two practice periods each week when he works alone, and after a year or two the supervised practicing should be discontinued, and the child should be able to study independently.)

This plan benefits everyone: the child gets along faster, the parent is relieved of the responsibility of getting the practicing done, the young teacher is gaining experience in teaching, and the older teacher has the satisfaction of helping the younger one in starting her career.

After some experience in supervising practicing, you can start to teach a pupil of your own. You will probably wish to continue to consult your own teacher, and to discuss your pupil's problems with her and, if possible, you will bring the pupil at regular intervals to play for her.

You would be wise to begin your career by teaching young children. As you grow in experience, your horizon will broaden, and your teaching schedule will become more diversified, and include older students as well.

With your growing experience, you will develop your own personal approach, dependent on your musical gifts and temperament. Your conception of what can be done at a music lesson will be continually enlarging. Always you will be following general teaching principles, but your teaching will become more flexible. Each lesson you give will be a new adventure for you as well as for the pupil. You will find that what worked with Susan at 3 o'clock may not necessarily be the best approach for teaching the same piece to Johnny at 4.

If possible, continue studying with a teacher yourself. But if this is not feasible, you can still keep up your study by constantly exploring and familiarizing yourself with more and more music. No matter how many pupils you teach, you have one most important and interesting pupil to educate for a lifetime, and that is yourself!

THE CHILD'S INDIVIDUAL
PIANO LESSON

The suggestions that follow are primarily concerned with lessons given to children, though the principles are the same for teaching students of all ages.

If we consider the amount of instruction that an eight-year-old child is given in most of the subjects he is studying, the time that is allotted to music lessons is comparatively very short. In many schools there are daily lessons in arithmetic, spelling, and reading. No parent would think that a child could advance rapidly in these subjects with only one lesson a week. But many parents *do* expect rapid advancement in the child's music study with only one short weekly lesson.

An ideal amount and distribution of time for a child's music study, it seems to me, is an hour a week class lesson in musicianship and an hour of individual piano instruction. Unfortunately, for a variety of reasons, this schedule is not always possible. Many children cannot give as much time as this to music lessons or perhaps the parents cannot afford the expense.

But if the child has only one piano lesson a week, no matter how long or how short it is, the teacher must plan carefully the best use of the precious lesson time, and her aim will be to make the lesson a valuable and varied musical experience for the child. The following subject matter should, if possible, be included in the curriculum: Technique, Sight Reading, Studying a New Piece, Reviewing an Old Piece, and Hearing Music in what I call "The Listener's Program." Of course, all of these subjects will not be covered in each piano lesson, but every piano student should be given this variety of musical experience. Variety is the spice of life, and it should be the spice of the music lesson!

VARYING THE ROUTINE

The student's curiosity will be aroused and his interest sustained if the order in which different subjects are taken up during the lesson time is varied.

Sometimes begin the lesson by sitting across the room from the piano, and ask the pupil to play a piece. This is the only way that you can check on what a child will do if asked to play at home. You will

12

find out whether he *can* play a piece "the first time," without any preliminary warming up with scales and exercises.

Sometimes start the lesson by working on the new piece that the pupil is studying, or start with teaching him a piece by rote.

Sometimes start with technique, or sight reading, or ear training — anything so that the pupil will not feel that a piano lesson always follows the same routine.

When I was a very young teacher, a five-year-old child made a remark that I considered most complimentary. I had entered a classroom of small children. The little chairs had been placed in an orderly row, and all but one were occupied, but a large pink rug that should have been removed was still on the floor, and Sally, a charming little girl, was sitting in the middle of it. Taking hold of one corner, I pulled the rug aside, with Sally coming along as a delighted passenger. She laughed with glee, and said, "I didn't know music lesson was going to be like this today!"

No two lessons, of course, will be the same. Yet teachers in discussing their methods of instruction often say, "*I make* my pupils do such and such"; "*I tell them* this or that"; or "*I always* do so and so." As you gain in experience, you will find that you cannot "make" people learn music, and the less you "tell" them, the more opportunity they will have for discovery. And, surely, because life is moving along and you yourself are learning all the time, you will not "always" do things the same way. Then you will find that these three words, "Make," "Tell," "Always," with their unfortunate connotations, are dropping from your vocabulary.

"Drives"

An experienced teacher will have an over-all plan of what she expects the pupil to accomplish during the year, and will refer to this frequently.

If the pupil is weak in a certain subject, it is sometimes a good idea to make a "drive" and spend most of the lesson time, or even a number of consecutive lessons, with the emphasis on this weak subject. Depending on the student you are teaching and what you are trying to help him to accomplish, the "drive" might be for memorizing, ear training, sight reading, or some other aspect of music study.

Recently in a lesson with an adult beginner who was discouraged because of her slowness in reading we spent all of our time in a "drive" for sight reading. By the end of the lesson, she had read fluently a number of easy pieces, keeping her eyes on the printed notes while she played, and saying aloud the time-values of the melodic line to keep herself going rhythmically. The pieces were so simple that she played them with confidence and accuracy. They sounded musical, and she was greatly encouraged. Taking all of one lesson to have her discover that she *could* read simple material fluently was far more important, at the moment, than hearing her play through the assignment she had been practicing.

GENERAL SUGGESTIONS FOR THE INDIVIDUAL PIANO LESSON

In any piano lesson, the matter of supreme importance is that the pupil shall *hear* every sound that he makes.

Technique, scales and exercises, should be an experience in listening. A pupil practices a succession of finger movements not primarily to acquire dexterity, but to be able to make a succession of beautiful sounds.

Sight Reading, too, should be an experience for the ear as well as for the eye. For instance, suppose a child is to read a measure containing a quarter note, a quarter rest, and a half note. He may think of it merely as something he does with his fingers, releasing the key on the second beat and holding the last note for two beats. This can be done with mechanical correctness, without his ears being engaged at all. But get him to *hear* the silence represented by the rest, and to *hear* that the tone of the half note is continuing through two beats. In the same way, he should listen with attention and interest to the sounds represented by dots and tied notes.

Usually I would play for a pupil the *New Piece* he is going to study. Many teachers feel that this is a mistake, fearing that the child will play by ear and will not learn to read. I do not share this view. Of course, every child must be studying sight reading continuously, but it has often seemed to me preferable that his first experience with a new piece should be to hear it as a whole, rather than to try to read it. If he is a poor sight reader, it might be a laborious ploughing through, which will give him no conception of the composition as a whole.

In presenting a new piece to study, the teacher should be sure that the student understands everything on the printed page. He should be familiar with the musical vocabulary of the piece, including the time values, phrasing, chords, and so on. If there is something in the piece with which he is not familiar, for example a new rhythmic figure using time values that he has not yet met, you can do one of four things:

1) You do not say anything about it, in which case it will probably come back the next week in a mess! or

2) you can play the figure for him, and have him learn it by imitation, in which case he is not understanding what he is doing, or

3) you can first show him the printed notes, then explain the arithmetical values, and finally have him play the figure, in which case you are not sure that he really hears what he is doing, or

4) — and this is probably preferable — you can teach it to him as follows: Before showing him the music, make up little melodic groups using the figure, and teach him by rote to play them on the piano, up the scale, until he is thoroughly familiar with the sound and the fingering. Then you can explain the arithmetic of the time values, and finally show him the notes on the printed page. They can now be introduced to him as the picture of the new friend whom he has just met. This order of learning insures that he will hear and understand completely what he sees, and he will probably play the figure correctly "the first time."

When you hear a pupil play his *Old Piece,* "in concert style," it is a good idea to have him play it straight through, without comment from you. Then, sometimes, ask him to tell you what parts sounded just as he wished. This sort of self-evaluation is important. In most instances, a student will begin by enumerating all the bad things that he did: he forgot to use the pedal, or his finger slipped, or he did not play G♯. But it is just as necessary for him to be aware of what he did well, as of what he did poorly.

The Listener's Program. The last few minutes of the lesson may be the most musically exciting of all. You can add more music to the situation than that which the pupil has prepared by playing some adult music for him. For instance, if a child has been playing the melody of "Twinkle, Twinkle, Little Star," you might play some of the variations that Mozart wrote on this melody. Or if a pupil has been playing a little waltz, play for him part of a Chopin waltz. Or if he is studying a Clementi sonatina and you have talked about the structure, play the exposition of the first movement of a sonata by Mozart or Haydn, where the structure is similar. (I remember as a young student, coming home from a piano lesson one day walking on air! I had played the Chopin B minor Prelude. At the end of the lesson, my teacher had played for me part of the B minor Scherzo, which I had never heard. Out of my limited experience, I had no idea that music could be like that. And it was hard for me to believe her when she told me that some day I too would be able to play that beautiful piece.)

Perhaps you can take a few minutes to play part of a phonograph recording of some orchestral or chamber composition written by the composer whose music your pupil has been studying.

Or you can have him learn to sing a grown-up song by ear. "Drink to Me Only With Thine Eyes" or "Passing By," or Schubert's "Heidenröslein," for example, can be learned easily by ear in a few minutes.

The last impression the student carries away with him from his lesson should be a musical one. Myra Hess, in a recent interview, spoke about piano teaching where the approach to music had been principally technical. "The student left the studio earth-bound," she said. To end the piano lesson with the student in contact with fine music insures that he will leave the studio "Heaven-bound"!

SOME PITFALLS IN THE PATH
OF THE YOUNG PIANO TEACHER

An experienced teacher who is musical and imaginative can, of course, give a clearer and better lesson than an inexperienced teacher, who may be equally gifted musically. The experienced teacher will have planned a well-organized lesson, and she will probably avoid the pitfalls into which the younger teacher might stumble. Here are a few of the pitfalls that can confuse and slow up a lesson.

Pitfall No. 1: The teacher assumes that the pupil knows something that he does not know.

It is difficult for a young teacher to realize that what she herself knows so well and what seems so obvious to her, may be a new and puzzling experience for the pupil. For instance, the new piece that you give him to learn may contain something that he has never seen and does not understand and that you have not explained to him. The rest of the piece may be completely within his experience and understanding, but the new thing that he does not know may cause confusion and discouragement in his mind, and he may think that the whole piece is too hard. The piece is not too hard! It is an easy piece, but it seems hard to him because one thing is unfamiliar.

A wise teacher will always go over the new piece carefully with the pupil before sending him home with the music, to be sure that he understands everything on the printed page. She will take nothing for granted.

An older woman once said to me, "So many teachers give their lessons the wrong week. If there were more lessons of Preparation, there would be no need for so many lessons of Correction."

Pitfall No. 2: The teacher may be *telling* the pupil too much, instead of helping him to discover for himself. A gifted teacher once summed it up by saying, "Teaching is not telling!"

Pitfall No. 3: A conscientious teacher who has planned a beautiful lesson may feel that she must go through the program that she has planned, regardless of the child's mood of the moment.

If a pupil comes to a lesson bursting with enthusiasm to study something that has not been assigned, by all means follow his musical

17

lead. For example, if he has been asked in school to play a march, certainly agree that he may learn one. Or if Mother's birthday comes next week, and he wants to learn to play "Happy Birthday To You," you will keep his musical interest burning by teaching him that most useful melody rather than by hearing all of the assigned lesson. No matter how carefully you have prepared the lesson, you should also be prepared to alter your plan if it seems advisable.

However, be sure that the pupil does not get the idea that the assignment you gave him last week is never going to be heard. Have him understand that you will be going back to it as soon as the music of immediate interest has been learned. It is very disconcerting to a pupil sometimes when the teacher does not "hear the lesson." He may wonder why in the world she asked him to practice it.

Pitfall No. 4:   The pupil may be discouraged and confused because the teacher has expected him to understand too much at one time. The young teacher, without realizing it, may be teaching two things at once. For instance, a piece to be studied may include a new rhythmic figure and also new notes to be learned.

But if the subject matter has been presented in small and consecutive steps, and each detail has been successfully accomplished, the student will be enjoying a series of small successes, and he will probably think that studying music is fun.

Pitfall No. 5:   Don't say "Don't!"

Here two negatives surely make an affirmative. A negative suggestion as to what *not* to do leaves the way open for every other possible action, good or bad. The classic example is that of the mother who said to the nursemaid, "Go into the garden and see what the children are doing, and tell them *not* to!"

Negative suggestions very often produce the exact opposite of the intended result. As soon as Bluebeard told his last wife not to go into a certain room, there was nothing in the world that she wanted more to do, this being the perversity of the human heart! The story of Pandora and even the story of the Garden of Eden illustrate this point. It is not a question of telling people what not to do, but of suggesting what they shall do, that is the true educational principle. The piano teacher's suggestion "Try to keep a light arm when you play staccato" is better than saying, "Don't let your arm be so heavy." "Play more slowly" is better than saying "Don't play so fast."

CHOOSING MUSIC FOR
CHILDREN TO STUDY

Our constant aim as piano teachers is to give our students an experience of music that has real and permanent cultural value. This is especially important in choosing the first music for children to study. We all know that much that we learn when we are very young we remember all our lives. Most grown-ups can still recite the nursery rhymes they learned as children. So we must be sure that the music we give children to learn is worth remembering.

FOLK MUSIC

Folk music fulfills this requirement and is, I think, the best possible material to use in forming a child's musical taste. Tunes like "Ach, du lieber Augustin," "Sur le Pont d'Avignon," "Frère Jacques," and "London Bridge is Falling Down" are well worth remembering. They have had sufficient vitality to stand the test of time, and have crossed many geographical frontiers. Tunes like these have been sung and played by countless children of many generations, and are remembered with pleasure by adults.

Folk music has been a source of inspiration to many composers. Both Brahms and Bartók did much research in this field, collecting and harmonizing many folksongs. Brahms made delightful arrangements of Hungarian dances, Dvořák of Slavonic dances, and there are the nineteen Hungarian Rhapsodies of Liszt.

Many composers have used folk music as the subject matter of their own works, developing it at length. Among the countless compositions stemming from folk music that come to mind are the Razumovsky String Quartets of Beethoven, the "Academic Festival Overture" of Brahms, D'Indy's "Symphony on a French Mountain Air," Vaughan Williams' "English Folk Song Suite," and the vast amount of Russian music from Balakirev to Khatchaturian. This list could, of course, be extended indefinitely.

Since folk music can be a source of inspiration to a composer, it will certainly furnish a sound basis for developing a child's musical taste. However, most of the folk music that children play will be folksongs,

19

written within the small compass of the singing voice. So, if the child is to gain pianism and freedom over the whole keyboard, folk music should be supplemented by other material, which should be chosen with care.

Easy Classics

Musically it is a simple and natural transition from the study of folk music to the study of the Easy Classics. Here there is a wealth of material: the little dances of Bach and Handel, the little pieces of Mozart and Beethoven, the children's pieces by Schumann, and many others.

In general, choose pieces with rhythmic appeal. For example, Bach is best introduced through the dances, not the Inventions, unless these can be taught interestingly by a teacher who can stimulate the child's curiosity about the contrapuntal style of writing.

In selecting editions of this music for children to study, choose those that are carefully phrased and fingered. For instance, Harold Bauer has edited the "Album for the Young" most carefully in his series of the complete Schumann piano works, published by G. Schirmer. The Diller-Quaile Solo Books, Numbers Two, Three, and Four, contain a number of Easy Classics which are phrased and edited with great care. These books contain pieces by the composers listed above, and also pieces in a wide variety of styles from Corelli to Grieg to Rebikov. The meaning of the music is clearly brought out by the editing.

In literature there is much written about children, or written to be read to children, that is too difficult for a child to read by himself. "The Wind in the Willows," "Winnie the Pooh," and "Charlotte's Web" are examples of this. So, in music, pieces like Debussy's "Children's Corner" and Schumann's "Scenes from Childhood" are written *about* children, and can be played *to* children, but they are certainly mature compositions, and not pieces to be taught to the average child.

Schumann's "Album for the Young," on the other hand, was written to be played by children, though these little pieces vary greatly in difficulty and maturity. "In Memoriam," for example, is distinctly an adult piece. But the collection also contains such familiar children's "classics" as "The Soldiers' March," "The Happy Farmer," and "The Wild Horseman."

Since we are building a musical foundation to last the student all his life, it would be a pity if he did not learn, while still young, some music that he will want to play as an adult. For example, the C major

Prelude from the first volume of "The Well-Tempered Clavier" is a piece that a young pianist can learn easily, and will enjoy playing as an adult. (May I register here a protest against Gounod's use of this composition! He published it as the accompaniment of a sentimental melody, set to the words of the *Ave Maria*, to be sung by a soprano, with a 'cello obbligato and an organ accompaniment thrown in. The other day I began playing the Prelude to a child who I thought might like to learn the piece, and she said, "Oh, that's the 'Ave Maria' that Roberta Peters sings!" . . . It seems to me that using music in strange ways is all very well for one's own entertainment, or for the amusement of one's friends. Myra Hess has a wonderful time playing the Chopin Black Key Etude by rolling a grapefruit around the keys of the right-hand part, while playing the left-hand chords. It is reported that she can also play the Pilgrims' Chorus with a whisk-broom! These amusing bagatelles, however, are strictly for home consumption.)

CONTEMPORARY MUSIC

In recent years, many composers have written music in the modern idiom especially for young pianists to play. Bloch, Bartók, Milhaud, Kabalevsky, Gretchaninoff, Alexandre Tansman, Roy Harris, and David Diamond, among others, have all written children's pieces in the modern idiom.

The language of music has changed and developed during the years, and many of the rhythms and sounds in contemporary music do not occur in folk music or in the easy classics. These sounds and rhythms have become part of the current musical vocabulary. The child is hearing them, and would probably enjoy learning to play some of these little pieces. In addition to the contemporary composers mentioned above, Octavio Pinto, Cecil Baumer, Frederic Hart, and Marcel Poot have written delightful music for children to play.

ARRANGEMENTS

Variety can be introduced into the child's repertory by giving him piano arrangements of familiar songs and themes of well-known symphonies. Much material of this kind has been published, but the teacher should be very careful to use only arrangements that have been made by experienced and sensitive musicians. And, of course, the arrangements should be faithful to the original music. Unfortunately, this is not always the case, as in the endeavor to bring the music within the child's reading ability and to fit his hand, the music is sometimes so simplified as to be unrecognizable.

I remember seeing in one book a succession of tones that could hardly be called a melody with the title, "Theme by Schumann." After considerable thought and use of the imagination, I concluded that these notes were all that was left of a melody from a Schumann symphony, after the arranger had completed his work of devastation! All of the rhythmic interest had been removed, many of the notes had been omitted, and the melody was completely dejected, and was left naked and shivering! The last person to recognize it would have been Schumann himself.

The pity of it is that a child learning such an arrangement gets the idea that this dull succession of sounds was really written by Schumann.

PRACTICAL REMINDERS

It is not wise to force a child to work on a piece that he definitely dislikes. There are plenty of pieces in the world to choose from, and nothing is gained by having a student of any age spend hours learning an uncongenial piece.

If a child is to learn a new piece, the teacher can perhaps play several for him at the lesson, and let him choose the one that he would like to study.

Most children love pieces that are printed in sheet music form, and often a child will learn a piece with pleasure if it is printed separately with a pretty cover, whereas he would not have been interested in learning the same piece if it were printed as No. 23 in a thick book.

FOUR BOOKS

Before closing this chapter, I would like to mention four books which may be of service to the young teacher. Three are books of Technique by Elizabeth Quaile; the fourth is a book of my own on Rote Teaching.

Miss Quaile's "First Book of Technical Exercises" was written to accompany the First Solo Book in the Diller-Quaile Series. The little exercises illustrate the principle of isolating a technical difficulty and playing it as a sequence up the scale. This procedure is valuable for familiarizing the child's hands with the gesture and the notes that are to be played, and is far more stimulating to the ear than practicing the notes over and over again on the same keys.

The two other books that Miss Quaile has written for elementary technique are called "Pre-Czerny, Books 1 and 2." These are full of suggestions on how to study technical passages. Instead of dwelling on the element of repetition, the emphasis is on analyzing the fundamental gesture and the rhythmic build-up of the passage—playing it first in its rhythmic outline, and gradually adding more and more notes. This is an excellent order of procedure in studying any technical passage, from these simple exercises to more complicated passages. The exercises are musical, short, and often amusing, and lead the student painlessly into the books of longer Czerny studies.

For teachers who are not familiar with teaching by rote, my own book may be helpful. It is called "Rote Teaching: What It Is and How To Do It." It contains nine small first-grade pieces, carefully analyzed, and with suggestions for teaching. Rote teaching is, of course, a supplement to, and not a substitute for, note reading, and insures that the child can quickly learn to play easily and correctly a piece which, at the moment, he could not possibly read.

GROUP TEACHING

Group work, as a supplement to the individual piano lesson, is advantageous to all concerned: the pupil, the teacher, and the parent.

Class work for young beginners can include the study of some of the fundamentals of music which all must know. These include notation of time-values and pitch, rhythmic design, phrasing, the formation of scales and chords, the meaning of Italian terms, etc. All of these can be easily learned by a group of pupils, while in the individual lesson each child uses the knowledge that he has gained in the class as it applies to the pieces that he is studying. In the class, children can begin creative work. The younger ones can supply original rhythmic or melodic answers to given phrases. Also they can make up tunes to words, or to given rhythmic patterns. Older children can study keyboard harmony and improvisation, and can compose their own little pieces which they can play and discuss in class.

The pupils have the fun of working with others, as they do in school. Often a child who would be reticent about singing or marching or clapping time-values alone in a "private" lesson will do these things naturally and easily in a class with other children.

Older pupils can sing chords in parts, which is an excellent way of experiencing harmony. Through singing rounds and canons, they can learn some of the elements of counterpoint; they can hear each other play the pieces that they have learned for the class to discuss; or, the teacher can play pieces that are too difficult for the children themselves to play, but that are within their musical comprehension.

The curriculum of class teaching can include listening to records of orchestral works; the students can follow the music with the piano score, and later, perhaps, with the orchestral score.

The advantages of group teaching to the teacher are obvious. She can give her pupils a broader music education than would be possible in a series of individual lessons. She is not teaching the same things over and over to a succession of individual pupils. Each pupil comes to the piano lesson with some knowledge of the music that he is studying, therefore she can devote more time to his playing and to his individual problems: perhaps technique, sight reading, or memorizing.

24

The success of class teaching depends very largely on the teacher's ability to keep every one in the room alert and interested. Conducting a class lesson is something like giving a party, with the teacher playing the part of the experienced hostess, who can keep track of all her guests and be constantly aware that each person is occupied and interested.

If, to the teacher, group work is a time-saver, to the parent it is a money-saver. For example, a teacher has four piano pupils, each of whom takes an individual hour lesson every week. With this schedule, she is, of course, teaching four hours a week, and each pupil receives an hour's weekly instruction. But if the teacher arranges her schedule so that each pupil has one three-quarter-hour piano lesson each week, and the four children come together for an hour's group work, each pupil is now receiving an hour and three quarters' weekly instruction. Since with this arrangement the teacher is still teaching only four hours a week, she can afford to give this instruction for the same fee that she would have charged for the four piano lessons of an hour each. Thus everyone is the gainer.

I realize, of course, that arranging such a schedule may be difficult to accomplish with children whose time is taken up with after-school activities, but it is well worth trying. Many teachers who believe that children up to seven years should have a year of group work in music before beginning to play an instrument, have been successful in carrying out this plan.

In my experience, the combination of group work and individual instrumental lessons can well be continued through the high school age and beyond. With adults, group teaching opens up a wide field of musical experience. This will be discussed later in this book.

MUSICIANSHIP AND
PIANO PLAYING

What do we mean by Musicianship? To my mind, its most important aspects are a recognition of the musical values in a composition and a sense of their relationship. Perhaps it can best be explained by an illustration.

Two children play the little Mozart F major Minuet. One child plays the piece like a well-trained pianist, the other like a musician. Both children play the right notes in proper tempo with the correct fingering. Both observe the phrasing that is indicated, and the other marks of expression. But there is a difference between the two performances, which can readily be heard. Wherein lies this difference?

The young pianist plays the notes of the piece correctly, and leaves it at that. It is a mechanical performance. The young musician, however, understands the music he is playing. His is a musical performance. He hears the quality of the different chords. He is aware that the piece has a recognizable structure, and that this structure must be projected in his playing. He is aware of the balance of the phrases and the relationship of the different parts of the piece.

The reader may say that this is a pretty tall order for an eight- or nine-year-old, and that this child must be unusually gifted. But any child, if he has a wise and musical teacher, can, from the beginning, learn to study music from the inside out, and can learn to use it as a language that he understands, and can give a musianly performance of even the simplest piece.

Of course, it is much easier to teach a piece of music than it is to write about how you teach it. But perhaps the following description of what a child can learn to hear in this little F major Minuet may be helpful.

First, before he has seen the notes, I would play the Minuet for him, to give him an idea of the piece. If he would like to learn it, I would tell him a little about Mozart. His father was a musician, and realized from the time that Wolfgang was three years old that the little boy was a musical genius. He composed this piece at the age of six.

Wolfgang had certainly seen and heard a great many minuets,

26

since there was much music going on in his home. I would talk about the minuet as a stately dance in 3 meter.

$$\frac{}{4}$$

Now I would have the pupil look over the printed music, and would help him to discover something of the structure of the piece, which consists of six four-measure groups (indicated by ⌐————————¬). The phrasing within each group is one measure, then one measure, then two measures. He will find that this grouping will be easily heard if, while he is learning the piece, he counts the number of beats in each phrase: that is, he can count "*One*-Two-Three, *One*-Two-Three, *One*-Two-Three-*Four*-Five-Six," instead of counting "*One*-Two-Three" for each measure. He will meet this grouping—two short phrases balanced by one that is twice as long—in many of the pieces that he will study.

If he has studied the formation of triads (which he certainly should have done by the time he is able to play this piece), he will recognize that most of the melody is made of broken chords. In the first measure he plays the F major triad, in the next, the B♭ major triad. If he has studied cadences, he will recognize that the third and fourth measures are a sort of variation of the chords I6 V I.

$$\frac{}{4}$$

He can sense the quality of the little cadence, with its suspension, and will hear that he is on the tonic triad, so, harmonically, he is back where he started in F major.

In the second group, however, Mozart is heading for a cadence on the dominant. The note he is interested in is, of course, C. He is like a little boy flying a kite. He plants his foot on C, and then watches the kite move higher and higher; first the tune goes up the chord C E G, then C F A, and finally, as the kite takes the wind and goes still higher, he puts in an extra note in a triplet C E G B♭. Then the melody turns downward, and with his second cadence, he is standing on the dominant triad, C major.

Mozart put a repeat sign after these first 8 measures.

In the next group, using a diminished seventh chord, Mozart makes a four-measure excursion into G minor. (Perhaps this is the first time that your pupil has met the sound of the diminished seventh chord. If so, you may want to digress for a few moments and show him how he can form this fascinating chord for himself, beginning on any key: for example, he can play C♯ with his right thumb, skip the next two keys, and play the third key, E, with the second finger; skip two more keys and play the third key, G, with his third finger; skip two more keys, and play the third key, B♭, with his fifth finger. All of this can be done simply by following the pattern *Skip, Skip, Play*, without bothering him with the letter-names of the notes. He will be hearing this chameleon-like harmony most frequently in all the music that he is going to play, especially when he arrives at playing Beethoven. Since the notes of the diminished seventh chord are all equidistant, it is one of the easiest chords to form on the piano. You can encourage him to experiment at home, forming diminished seventh chords beginning on any key, black or white, that he wishes. Later he will learn the many resolutions of the chord.)

In the little Minuet, the diminished seventh chord leads him at once into the G minor triad, and he is adventuring into a darker little harmonic bypath, with a cadence in G minor.

Then, in the next group the harmonies are brighter, as with a sequence he comes back once again to F major. Get him, if possible, to hear the difference in color between the diminished seventh chord, F♯ A C E♭, in the earlier group and the bland chord, E G B♭ D, in the first measure of the later group, resolving into F major.

There is still more to be said! The child Mozart, with his instinctive sense for form, proceeds to repeat the melody of the first four measures, slightly altering the bass in the first two measures. He must have been happy, and perhaps amused, when he thought of ending the group this time with D in the bass, which he marks with an impressive fermata. Later your pupil will learn that this surprising effect is called a Deceptive Cadence.

Then Mozart says to himself, "We really must stop all this meandering, and go home to F major, where we started." So, he plays the opening tune once more, and ends with an Authentic Cadence squarely in F major.

This little Minuet is truly a remarkable piece for a young child to have composed, and is a wonderful example of musical intuition and feeling for perfect balance.

After your pupil has practiced the piece, and can play it comfortably, there are other points of structure that he can investigate: for example, he can compare the six little cadences, with their turned-up or turned-down suspensions. Also, he may play the last measure in each of the six phrases, in succession, out of context, to notice how these cadences are balanced, and to hear how they rhyme. He may be surprised to realize that the melody of four of the six cadences ends with the same notes, the upward curve E to F. One other cadence curves upward, F♯ to G, and only one (the second) curves down, A to G.

You may call his attention to the pull of the dissonant notes against the chords, as each suspension resolves.

Minuet

The above description of the little Mozart Minuet is not given in any sense as a prescription of how this piece *should* be taught, but rather as a springboard for the teacher's own thinking. And, of course, the pupil will not discover all these things during his first lesson on the piece. Children vary in their pace of learning, depending on their temperament and their intelligence, and whereas one child may learn to play this piece in a week, another may take two or three weeks to learn it. The discussion of the structure of the piece will accordingly be spaced over the period of time it takes the child to learn to play the Minuet.

However, at the first lesson on any piece, I would take up the question of pianistic style. Surely a sense of style is an element in musicianship. With the Mozart Minuet, for example, I would explain to the child that this minuet was probably written for an instrument that had a light and delicate action, so the piece should be played lightly and delicately. If he plays with a light arm and clean finger articulation, he will probably produce the quality of tone that the piece demands.

If your pupil's ears and imagination and intelligence have been stirred, he will be able to play this little piece as beautifully as it can be played.

*   *

*

Combining musicianship with piano playing should begin at the pupil's first lesson. If a child can learn in his earliest lessons that music is something to be investigated by him, and that he is to make discoveries about every piece that he plays, his musical education will begin on a sure foundation. Musicianship and pianism always go hand in hand, and we wish our students to develop not only as pianists, but as true musicians.

Of course, the vocabulary that you will use in talking about music will vary with the age and experience and intelligence of the student. In a lesson you give an older student, you may use more technical terms, but you will still make musicianship the heart of every lesson.

What we are always trying to do with students of any age is, of course, to stimulate their curiosity.

I remember an older student who came to play for me. She had played notes for years in an accurate but pedestrian fashion. She was unaware that there was any special sense to the sounds that were produced by her very facile fingers. It took some time to get her to stop and listen and hear what she played. Little by little she became intrigued with the structure of the music that she studied. One day she was reading a Beethoven sonata that she was going to learn. As she turned the page, she said, "Well, let's see what's going on here." And at this point I said, "Your musical education has just at this moment begun because at last your curiosity has been aroused."

Musicianship is most emphatically not a collecting of musical facts about a piece, or merely identifying such elements of structure as chords or modulations. In its broadest sense it is an awareness of the relationships within the piece itself. Perhaps this awareness is the most important part of the performer's interpretation.

The parts of a composition are not separate entities, held together by musical "safety-pins." The parts are inwardly related. They form a complete organism, just as do the parts of the human body. The recognition of these inner relationships is vital to the understanding of any piece of music.

All poets and all philosophers deal with values and their relationships, and so do musicians. The English poet, Francis Thompson, spoke most eloquently when he said, in "The Mistress of Vision,"

> All things . . .
>
> Near or far
>
> Hiddenly,
>
> To each other linked are.
>
> That thou canst not stir a flower
>
> Without troubling of a star.

PURELY PRACTICAL

The Teacher's Studio

The following suggestions for the set-up of the teacher's studio are so obvious that I hesitate to mention them here, but they may perhaps be useful as a reference list.

Equipment

A *Piano* with easy action is desirable. Of course, it should be well tuned at all times. A second piano can be used to great advantage in teaching keyboard harmony and ear training, for teaching "touch" by imitation from one piano to the other, for adding second piano parts to children's solo pieces, and is, of course, indispensable for ensemble playing.

Piano Chairs or Benches should be adjustable as to height. *Footstools* and *Cushions* will be needed so that small children can sit comfortably at the piano.

If possible, the teacher should have in the studio a *Phonograph* and a well-selected library of *Records;* also a library of *Music* and *Books on Music.* This should certainly include, for quick reference, a Dictionary of Musical Terms, and a Biographical Dictionary of Musicians.

To avoid the necessity of students having to buy music that they will use only occasionally, the teacher, if possible, should supply copies of the music for analysis.

Gadgets

The *Metronome* should be used sparingly! (See page 93.)

Among the many gadgets on the market, I find the *Wright Note Finder* a useful aid in teaching sight reading.

For little children, I have used the *Eye-Hi Music Rack,* an ingenious device that brings the music down to any desired level, and keeps little children from the strained position of having to look far up to the printed notes.

A model of a *Piano Key* including the hammer and damper can be purchased from most of the piano manufacturers, and is of interest in demonstrating piano action.

For Class Work: Wooden Keyboards with raised keys; a *Blackboard* with painted staves; soft *Chalk* that will make note heads with a single stroke; *Erasers.* These will all be needed in the classroom.

Each student should have a book of manuscript paper and a notebook, preferably loose-leafed.

Arrangement of the Room

For class work, plan the geography of the room so that the children will be seated with their backs to the door—then they will not look up when anyone enters the room. If possible, arrange the seats so that the light comes from the side or from above. Plan the seating so that each student has a direct view of both the blackboard and the piano keyboard. The student who is seated at the piano should be able to see what may be written on the blackboard.

THE TEACHER'S NOTEBOOK

It is a good idea to keep a notebook in which you record at the beginning of the teaching season the work that you can reasonably expect each of your pupils to cover during the year. There should be a page or pages for each pupil, giving in some detail the work to be done, perhaps under the following headings:

1. *Technique,* listing the scales, arpeggios, exercises, or etudes to be learned.
2. *New Pieces* to be learned.
3. *Reading Material.*
4. *Old Pieces* to be reviewed.
5. *Creative Work.*

Then might come a list of the subjects in which the student is weak and which you will want to stress: perhaps his sight reading, or memorizing, or ear training, or establishing good practicing habits.

As the year progresses, you may wish to make a list of the pieces that the student has studied and played well.

THE TEACHER'S LESSON PLAN

An experienced teacher will organize in her mind the lesson that she is going to give, possibly making a brief outline of the subject matter. However, a subject you thought you could cover in 15 minutes may take half an hour, so your lesson plan must always be flexible to meet the situation of the moment. But with a plan in mind, at least you are not teaching in a haphazard fashion.

It is also helpful to make notes, directly after a student's lesson,

of points that you want to be sure to take up in the following lesson
—else you may forget them.

In planning your teaching schedule, it is a good idea to have a
5-minute interval between consecutive lessons. This will give you a
chance to make your notes for future reference on the lesson you have
just given, to organize your thoughts, and also to get yourself musically, mentally, and emotionally prepared to meet the next student.
If you are going to teach a piece by rote in the following lesson,
it may be wise to play the piece over once during the 5-minute
interval to be sure that you have it firmly in mind and that you
remember exactly the steps you will take in teaching it. (My own
book, "Rote Teaching: What It Is and How To Do It," contains
detailed suggestions of procedure.)

The Pupil's Notebook

It is advisable for the pupil to have a notebook in which either
he or the teacher writes the assignment for the next lesson. And
some children like to keep in their notebook a record of the amount
of time that they have practiced.

On the last page of the notebook the pupil can make a list
of the pieces he has memorized and played really well. The list
may be headed "Repertory" or "Concert Pieces." Then, when a
student is asked to review an old piece, it can be selected, either
by the pupil or the teacher, from this list.

If during the lesson you play some adult music for the pupil
to hear, he can list in his notebook the names of the pieces you
play under a heading such as "Listener's Program."

The teacher may sometimes write in the pupil's notebook reminders
of special matters that have been stressed in the lesson. For instance,
for a pupil who was using the pedal for the first time, I once wrote,
"Keep your ear on what your right foot is doing." And for a pupil
playing with a stiff arm, "Keep your arm as light as a feather. Let
your upper arm travel opposite to where your hand is playing." And
for a pupil working on sight reading, "Keep your eyes on the notes
and always look ahead!"

Notebooks for Class Work

In group teaching of adults, notebooks are so essential that one
hardly needs mention them.

The writing of notes while a lesson is in progress should, of course, be an art of selection and compression. However, sometimes you will find that some of the students in a group are trying to write down as fast as they can everything you say, thereby losing entirely the continuity of the lesson.

I remember an amusing instance of indiscriminate note-taking by a teacher who was visiting a class of 12-year-olds whom I was introducing to a new chord formation. The visitor inadvertently left her notebook in the classroom. There was no name on the book, and I was unable to trace its ownership. But I was rather horrified to read her last observation, which was, "The children are bright, but she goes very fast, and if the first one doesn't get it, she goes right on to the next one."

The owner of the notebook did not learn as much from her note-taking as I did myself from that remark!

Sometimes you can control the indiscriminate taking of notes by saying, "Will you please listen and not write." Another time you might say, "Will you please write the following note from my dictation."

When you dictate to a group, some students, of course, will write more rapidly than others, and the slow ones will be hopelessly confused if you talk too hurriedly. You can adjust the speed of your dictation by watching the hands of the writers. When you see that the slowest hand has stopped writing, you will know that this is the moment to continue dictating.

ON MARKING LESSONS

Sometimes little children are happy if, after they have played a piece well, the teacher affixes a little gold or silver star in the margin next to the piece. And some children like to have their lessons marked with letters or numbers.

In one school where I taught there was a large chart in the waiting room. It was headed "Practice Record." The lesson dates were printed on the top line, and a list of the children's names was printed vertically on the left margin. If the week's practicing had been well done and the lesson was satisfactory, the teacher would affix a silver star opposite the child's name and under the date. If the performance had been superlative, there was a gold star. If the child had been absent, this was indicated by "a." And if the work was not satisfactorily done, no mark at all was indicated.

Since children are accustomed to having their school lessons marked, sometimes a child may like to have his music lessons marked also. If he does, and if marks are a stimulus to him, there is no harm in using them. But the child should understand that the mark is not something you give him, but something that he has earned. It is your estimate of his effort and achievement, and a record of his own accomplishment. Be careful that he does not work primarily for the mark. After the lesson, you can discuss with the pupil how he thinks it went. Was it worth an A or a B? This will help the child to be self-evaluating, and will help him judge his own achievement.

On the other hand, if marking a lesson discourages a child, or if it makes no difference to him, there is no point in using marks. Particularly in class work, marking can sometimes be a very disheartening practice, because it fosters competition, and competition—though it may be the life of trade—has nothing to do with the study of music! Children in a group probably compare their marks, and this will discourage the slower and less gifted children of the group. A's and A+'s may be stimulating to bright children, but for children who are not so bright, B's and C's may not only discourage them from making further efforts to study, but may even make them dislike the subjects in which these marks were given them.

The attitude of Parents toward marking lessons is discussed on page 159.

In general, the whole question of marking lessons should be treated with sensitivity and sympathy.

THEN AND NOW

Had this chapter been written some fifty years ago, when I began teaching, the account of what went on in the average piano lesson would have been quite different from what it is today.

At that time little attention was given to the study of music itself. The piano teacher's afternoon usually consisted of hearing one child after another play exercises and perform pieces.

I remember a questionnaire that was sent to a large number of teachers about that time, asking how long their pupils continued piano lessons. I quote the results of this survey of "pupil mortality."

Less than 45% of pupils continue their studies after the first three months.

90% stop taking lessons before reaching the 3rd grade of piano music.

What was the reason for this? Music was surely as exciting an experience then as it is now! In looking back, it seems to me that the cause of the trouble was two-fold: in the first place, the curriculum that was provided was so limited and dull that even the musical child could not be interested in it; in the second place, many of the teachers were untrained and unimaginative and so could not arouse the child's interest or curiosity, and there was little joy in the lessons for either teachers or pupils.

I was reminiscing about this recently with an elderly friend, a noted patron of music, who told me of her own piano lessons as a child. Her teacher "came to the house," and the lessons were of the most Spartan variety. The teacher seemed more interested in what she considered correct hand position than in any other aspect of her teaching. She was armed with a formidable ruler. The fashion of the day was to play the piano with depressed knuckles, and if the pupil's knuckles were raised anywhere near to normal position, the ruler came down with considerable force.

My friend told me that on one wintry day she looked out of the window and saw the teacher approaching on the slippery path leading to the house. She so hated her music lessons, she said, that she prayed the teacher would slip on a piece of ice and break her neck! My friend is a gentle soul, and I was astonished at this vehement recital of her childish reaction to piano lessons, and surprised that after all these years she could speak with such heat about her first contact with music.

Fortunately, she grew up to be an ardent music lover. But how many adults there must be who have given up all interest in music because their first teachers were unimaginative and unsympathetic, and the musical diet was so sparse! And how many more there are who still love music, but have given up all hope that they can ever play the piano and make music themselves, because they are haunted by the fact that they once took lessons that did not "take"!

Playing by ear was completely discouraged fifty years ago. Another elderly friend told me that as a child of five, she was constantly making up little pieces and playing tunes by ear on the piano. Her family thought she was musical and should have piano lessons, but her teacher told her that it was "wrong" to play by ear, and that she must read everything she played. By the time she was eight, the flow of original pieces had stopped. She had entirely lost the desire and the ability to play by ear, and this she never regained.

Similarly, a famous artist, in speaking of a child's creative desire to paint, once said that if by the time a child is eight years old this desire has had no outlet or has been thwarted, the "iron curtain" will fall on the creative spirit, and may never rise again.

John Dewey has made a noteworthy contribution to our ideas of the inherent capacity of children to create and to express themselves in many fields. One of these is the field of music. Progressive music teachers have taken to heart his famous phrase, "Learning by Doing." Children are now encouraged to create their own rhythms and melodies, and the modern teacher knows that teaching music entirely by the book is a thing of the past. Beginning in the kindergarten, children are taught rhythm through the use of their bodies, and through playing in a rhythm band; they learn to sing, they learn to listen to music, they learn to create their own music. They learn by doing.

Piano teaching has certainly changed greatly since the turn of the century! Nowadays, piano students, besides being taught how to play the instrument, are also educated as musicians.

The music that children are given to play nowadays is infinitely more varied than formerly. As was said before, many of our important composers have written music especially for children, and the market is flooded with "Methods" designed to make the musical pathway of the young pianist agreeable and entertaining.

Children also have many more opportunities to hear music than formerly. All over the country there are concerts especially planned for children, and in many cities there are performances of operas and chamber music for young audiences. Innumerable recordings have been made especially for children.

In every way, the child's musical horizon has broadened immeasurably.

CONCLUSION

The teacher works with each pupil in a field much broader than the one that is bounded by the music that the pupil can play. Encourage your students to hear music whenever possible, and you can increase their interest by discussing with them the music they have heard.

Your own musical enthusiasm is perhaps your principal asset, and this should always be so strong and constant as to be contagious. In the last analysis, in the pupil-teacher relationship, as in any relationship, the greatest thing you have to give is yourself.

All told, teaching music is a continually refreshing profession. It is highly recommended!

Part III. Teaching Accompanied By Learning

James Harvey Robinson began a lecture on Teacher Training at Columbia University several years ago by remarking in his slow, drawling voice: "As I go around the country, visiting schools and colleges, I am surprised at the great amount of teaching that is being done, entirely unaccompanied by learning."

The phrase struck me so forcibly that I have never forgotten it. From it I have derived the title of this section.

The chapters in this section can be grouped under the general heading "How To." Some of these How To's are suggestions addressed to the teacher. Others are addressed directly to the student.

PHRASING

INTRODUCTION

Phrasing lies at the very heart of interpretation. The words "Phrase" and "Phrasing," however, are used in so many senses that their meaning is often ambiguous. For example, according to one definition, a phrase consists of an even number of measures, two, four, or eight. According to another, a phrase is a group of notes that is marked with a slur and is to be played legato.

In discussing any subject, it is clarifying to begin by defining one's terms. I am using the word Phrase as meaning any succession of tones that conveys a recognizable musical idea and so can be called a music-unit. A phrase may be long or short. It moves in unbroken continuity toward some more or less definite point. This curving arrow ⟶ is a picturesque sign* that expresses the forward movement and also shows the length of the phrase.

---

* This sign is used extensively in Tobias Matthay's illuminating book, "Musical Interpretation," published by Joseph Williams Ltd. in London.

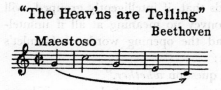

"The Heav'ns are Telling"
Beethoven
Maestoso

Sonata Op. 57 (2nd movement)
Beethoven
Andante con moto

Sonata Op. 10, No. 2
Beethoven
Allegro

Compare the endings of the three phrases quoted above. In the first example, the curving arrow extends through the note C; in the second example, it extends through the dot; and in the third example, it extends through the rest.

As to the word Phrasing, an excellent definition is that of Hubert Foss, who defines it as "The art of the expressive grouping of musical sounds." Here he is saying that grouping is implicit in phrasing. His use of the word "expressive" implies that phrasing includes sensitivity to the dynamics inherent in the phrase, as well as awareness of the melodic curves and the harmonic meanings. These points are discussed at length in the present chapter.

We will begin our investigation of phrasing by discussing grouping.

THE GROUPING OF TONES OR OF WORDS

To my mind, the phrasing of tones bears the same relationship to expressing the meaning of music as does the grouping of words to the meaning of English or any other spoken language.

In English, a succession of words that, if intelligently grouped, will convey intelligible meaning, may convey no meaning at all if unintelligently grouped. For example, read the opening words of Hamlet's soliloquy, grouping them as follows:

"To be *or,* not to be *that,* is the question *whether.*"

If the sentence is read with the grouping as indicated above, it has a delightful rhythm and sounds rather profound, but is, of course, utter nonsense. The trouble is caused by pausing in the wrong places, that is, by grouping together successive words that do not belong together. Stressing the wrong words also contributes to the confusion.

Similarly, in music, a melody can be distorted by unintelligent grouping. For example, if the tune of "My Country, 'Tis of Thee" were phrased as indicated by the arrows in the following illustration, it would be a caricature of the melody. It is as unintelligible to group the tones in this way as it is to group the words in the Shakespeare quotation as suggested above.

I remember once when I was giving a course on musical analysis to a group of college professors, I played the theme of a Bach fugue we were about to study, and said, "This is the way the theme is phrased."

A teacher of Spanish asked, "But how do you know you are right?"

I asked him, "In one of your own classes, if a student was reading aloud something in Spanish, how would you know whether he understood what he was reading, or was only pronouncing correctly a succession of words?"

He replied, "I understand the Spanish language, and could hear by the way he read whether he understood it or not."

"It is exactly the same with music," I said. "If you understand the language of music, when it is being performed you will hear whether the performer does or does not understand what he is playing. As we have said, one of the most important elements in conveying meaning in any language is through the phrasing."

The Spanish teacher conceded that this was a valid analogy.

In the printing of a spoken language, a variety of punctuation marks — commas, semicolons, periods, etc. — is used to help the reader's eye to see at once the grouping of the words, and thus to apprehend the meaning of what he is reading. But there are few such marks in printed music. It is comparatively easy for a composer to write down certain elements of the musical ideas that he has in mind so that they will be understood by everyone. Time-values, pitch of notes, dynamics, and tempo can be indicated. But a composer cannot indicate all of the structural grouping of the music he writes. He cannot indicate all of the phrasing. He must rely on the sensitive ear of the performer and his familiarity with the language of music.

How the Groups are Articulated

In speaking English or in playing music, how do we articulate the phrasing? How do we group the words or the tones so that the meaning may be clear?

In speech we find that we make a slight pause after the last word of a phrase. And in music we lengthen very slightly the ending of a phrase. The pause or lengthening may be very short, but is sufficiently definite to keep the phrases from running together.

We unconsciously use this technique in everyday speech. Orators, preachers, radio commentators, all addressing an audience, emphasize phrasing in their delivery. We are all familiar with Edward R. Murrow's introductory sentence as he begins his illuminating commentary on the events of the day: "This [Pause] is the news. [Longer Pause]." Then he proceeds to tell us what has happened in the world, and his brilliant analysis is always easy to follow because of his unfailingly lucid phrasing.

In reading the following lines of poetry, you will notice that you will instinctively make a slight pause after the last syllable of each little group as indicated by the arrows. The longer arrows indicate the larger groups:

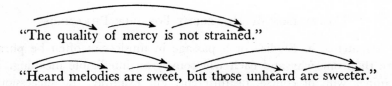

"The quality of mercy is not strained."

"Heard melodies are sweet, but those unheard are sweeter."

Similarly, in playing a legato melody, the pianist can indicate the phrasing by the slightest lengthening of the sound at the end of each little grouping. The lengthening of this sound is delicate and subtle, and is not long enough to disturb the over-all line of the rhythm or the continuity of a legato melody. But it does articulate the phrasing and make the musical meaning clear by keeping the phrases from running together in a metrical sing-song. For example, the beginning of the

Pilgrims' Chorus from Wagner's opera "Tannhäuser" is grouped as follows:

We hear that the shorter notes are moving toward the longer ones, the quarters are moving toward the halves in the first two little groups. And the time values in the last two measures keep the melody moving continuously to the end of the phrase.

If the last note of a group is staccato, or if the group ends with a rest, the silence at the end can be slightly lengthened. For example, here is the beginning of the melody of the Scherzo movement from Beethoven's Ninth Symphony:

In this melody, of course, no lengthening of tones is possible, since all are played staccato. But the articulation of each measure, as indicated by the arrows, conveys the obvious meaning of the passage.

COMPARISON OF DIFFERENT POSSIBLE PHRASINGS

A sentence in English or a passage in music can often be phrased more than one way and each will convey an intelligible meaning. The meanings will, of course, be different. For example, the succession of words, "Woman without her man is a menace" can be read in two ways. If you pause after the words "Woman," "man," and "menace," you convey one meaning:

"Woman,   without her man,   is a menace!"

But if you pause after "Woman," and "her," and "menace," you will have voiced the opposite idea:

"Woman,   without her,   man is a menace!"

The succession of words contained the two different meanings all the time. These different meanings were conveyed through the phrasing, that is, the pauses indicating the ends of the groups of words came in different places.

An amusing instance of the significance of Pause is a comparison between the two words "Welfare" and "Farewell." In each case, the stressed syllable is "well" ("Wel"). The sound of this syllable is the same, although the spelling is different. So the change of meaning is not a matter of accent.

Repeat each word two or three times. Notice that when you say "Welfare," you will instinctively make a slight pause after "fare," the last syllable. But when you say "Farewell," the pause is after the "well," now the last syllable. Ask someone to listen to you while, without stopping, you repeat these words: "Welfare welfare welfare well farewell farewell farewell." If your listener can hear when you change from one word to the next, he is instinctively recognizing that the pause is coming in a different place and that the meaning is changing. He is hearing your phrasing.

Similarly, in music, a passage may often be phrased in different ways and will convey different, but perfectly intelligible, meanings. The following examples illustrate this point:

1) Bach G major Minuet

Either of these phrasings makes musical sense.

2) Handel Corrente

These little phrases are played staccato, so there is, of course, no lengthening of the last tone of the group. But the groupings are clearly audible if in the two-note phrases the slightest pause is made after the second of the notes.

3) Trio from Minuet in G of Beethoven

The Trio has been printed with the phrasings as indicated in the first example. The reason for the second grouping is that it makes apparent these details:

   a) The ear can hear the "rhyming" of the two D's at the end of each downward movement.

   b) The cross rhythm of the four-note descending figure in E minor played immediately as a sequence in D major.

4) Nocturne in F minor, Op. 55, No. 1, Chopin

The melody might be phrased, following the chords, in two different ways:

5) "In Memoriam" of Schumann

The first example is the first two measures of the piece. The second example is measures 19 and 20. The melodic line is the same, but there is no question that there are points of difference in the grouping of the tones within the phrase.

In the first example, the first little three-note group extends through the C♯ because of the underlying A-major harmony. The second note, D, is, of course, a passing note linking E with C♯ in the A-major chord. In the second example, Schumann harmonizes the E and D as a cadence in D major, so D is here the end of the first little group. This is followed by C♯ and B, here harmonized as a cadence in B minor, with B the end of the next little group.

In the first example, at letter B, the appoggiatura A resolves to G♯ in the dominant seventh chord. In contrast, in the second example, the appoggiatura A resolves delightfully to G♯ on a tentative diminished seventh chord. Play these two passages in succession, listening to the charming variety in the phrasing, produced by the different har- monizations.

How to Study Phrasing

The question is often asked: "How do you decide on the correct phrasing of a passage?" An excellent way to study the phrasing of a passage is as follows:

First play the passage straight through, as nearly up to time as you can, in order to get the general sense. Then start at the beginning, still playing up to time, but now stop on the tone that your ear tells you is the last note of each phrase, no matter how short the group. It may be a figure of two notes, or it may be more than a measure that your ear tells you makes sense, and is to be heard as a music-unit. In this kind of study, end with a prolongation of the last sound: that is, do not end with a staccato note, or with a rest, even though they may be indicated in the music and eventually you will play the passage this way. The idea is for you to follow the articulation of the groups by exaggerating the length of the last tone. If you do this throughout an entire passage, stopping at the end of each group, your ear will recognize that you are making musical sense.

In the final performance, of course, these prolongations are reduced to a minimum, so as not to interfere with the over-all line of the rhythm, but your ears hear and your fingers feel these articulations no matter how swiftly you will eventually play the piece.

It is important in investigating the phrasing of a passage to play each of the groups at approximately the speed of the final performance. In other words, you play phrases of quick notes, but play the phrases in slow succession.

It is the same principle that a pianist once told me he employed in acquiring finger dexterity. He said, "You must make very quick motions, but in slow succession, so that you can realize what you have done. You do not make slow motions in quick succession, which is a most boring use of one's time at the piano, and cannot lead to rapid playing. What you are aiming for, of course, is to play quick notes in quick succession! So, from the beginning of your practicing, learn to make quick motions!"

We will illustrate this way of investigating the phrasing of a passage with the beginning of the Gavotte from Bach's G major French Suite. Play the following quotation up to time, but make a prolongation of the last tone of each group, as indicated by the fermatas.

The effect is, of course, highly exaggerated, but you will hear that the tune makes sense. Your ear instinctively recognizes the similarity between these groups (a, b, c). Then play the passage up to time, eliminating the exaggerated fermatas, but clearly articulating the phrasing.

All of the following quotations should be studied by the same procedure as suggested above.

The phrasing of the beginning of the C major Invention of Bach seems to be organized as follows:

Notice that the little groups are of varying lengths, as indicated by the curving arrows.

In the Carl Philipp Emanuel Bach Solfeggietto, with its continuous movement of groups of four sixteenth notes, the phrasing follows a familiar pattern. The rhythmic grouping is indicated not by fermata signs but only by curving arrows. Your ear will recognize that each rhythmic unit ends on the first sixteenth of the metrical group.

In the Bach F major Invention, each group has as its objective the note that comes at the beginning of the beat.

Notice the melody that is made by playing in succession the terminal notes of each group:

Other examples of grouping are printed below.

In each case, movement is achieved by "following through" to the end
of the figure.

REDUCING A PASSAGE TO ITS HARMONIC BASIS

As we have seen, the recognition of harmony and harmonic progressions is one of the factors in phrasing. In studying phrasing, it is
helpful to reduce passages to their simplest rhythmic and harmonic
terms. First play a passage as written, then play it in a reduction to its
simplest form, finally play it again in the original form.

The following examples show passages written in broken chord form.
They are then printed in reduction, with the tones played simultaneously,
so that the student may hear clearly the movement of the chord masses.

In the Mozart C major Sonata, K. 545, comes this passage:

The passage can be reduced to a succession of solid chords as follows —
thus giving a clear idea of the phrasing of the sequence pattern:

Another example of music written in broken chords is the flamboyant C major Etude, Op. 10, No. 1, of Chopin. Here is the beginning as originally written, and in a chord reduction:

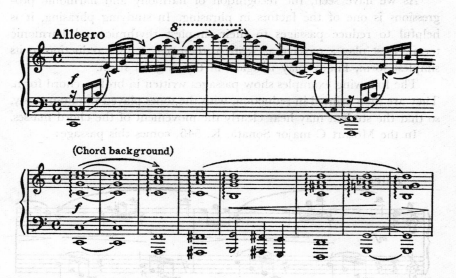

Notice that underneath the swiftly moving arpeggios in sixteenth notes there is a steady slow-moving harmonic organization of chords in whole notes. If the piece were played with an orchestral accompaniment, the chord background might be played by the orchestral instruments, while the piano is playing the sweeping arpeggios that Chopin wrote. In reducing the passage this way, the student will hear that this chord background is an integral element of the composition, and that the phrasing is intrinsic in the movement of the chords.

As we have seen, the process of reduction may involve simplifying the time-values and the arrangement of the chord notes, and removing non-harmonic tones. A musical phrase can doff its decorations, and the harmonic framework on which the phrasing rests will be more

apparent. For example, the Chopin Waltz in A-flat, Op. 69, No. 1, is
written as follows:

This passage can be reduced to:

Another example of removing non-harmonic tones to hear chord structure is the Turkish Rondo of Mozart, given below:

It is interesting to discover what is taking place in this tune, and to compare the delicate little dissonances. The melody begins by leaping up the A minor triad in a series of turns, each one commencing with an appoggiatura on the beat. We hear the little downward pull of these tones as each resolves to the chord note below, and we hear the little upward pull of the lower tone, as the turns complete themselves. Then the pattern changes completely. We now hear the chord notes B and G coming directly on the beat over the E minor triad. The non-harmonic passing tone A connects the two tones. Then the melody, on its way to E, runs down from B to F♯, the tones being connected with passing notes A and G. The ear should be aware of the delicate differences between the non-harmonic tones that come on the beats, and those that do not. That is, the ear must register the difference between appoggiaturas and passing notes. Hearing or not hearing all of these details affects your phrasing of the passage!

Play the following illustration very deliberately, and compare it with the original. Notice all that is happening to the note B in the three harmonic situations of the original. First B pushes its way into the A minor triad, then becomes the brilliant fifth of the E minor triad, and finally the assertive dominant note that moves us into the new key.

In playing the passage as Mozart wrote it, be sure that you hear these changes as you go along.

It seems to me that often we do not listen enough to what we are playing, nor do we think enough about it. Attention to these details helps to secure an interesting performance, and certainly makes for easier listening.

Another illustration of reducing a passage to its basic chord structure is the Chopin F minor Etude. The melody consists of chord tones, each surrounded by a delicate and lovely filigree of non-harmonic tones. If the melody is studied, making a prolongation of the last tone of each phrase, the harmonic structure will be clearly heard. Here are the first four measures.

The following is a possible reduction of the passage. The non-harmonic tones in the first two measures of the melody are decorating C. In the third measure E♮ and B♭ are similarly decorated, and in the fourth measure, C and A♭.

The phrasing of a passage containing suspended tones can be studied by reducing it to its simplest chord structure. For example, a chain of suspensions expresses musically a series of harmonic resistances. The chords are moving at the expected speed, but the melodic notes are holding back, and one feels a succession of moments of tension, followed by the satisfaction of the tension having been released. The following passage from the Mozart G major Sonata K. 283 illustrates this point. Here is the passage as Mozart wrote it:

Allegro

Frequently one hears this played strictly in time, in a sort of "um-pah, um-pah" performance, as though the player were counting "One-and-, Two-and" (which unfortunately is often the case!). This gives no idea of the real meaning of the passage. To hear the meaning of the suspensions, play the passage as follows in a harmonic reduction:

Then play it again as Mozart wrote it, but this time lengthen the first half of each beat until your ear is aware that this is the moment of resistance. The left hand note plays alone, and the right hand note is holding back until the pull of the bass is so strong that the melody tone loses its balance and follows the direction in which the bass is moving.

It is something like an adult holding a reluctant child by the hand, and pulling him past the fascinating window of a toy shop!

Here is another quotation of a chain of suspensions written in the original form, and then in reduction: it is from the Bach E major Invention:

The Bach Invention appears as written in the first illustration. Then, in the first reduction, the suspensions are omitted, but the passing note structure remains. In the second reduction the passage appears only as a series of chord tones.

The Schumann "Albumleaf" is another example of reducing suspensions:

Every aspect of the organization of music can be regarded as an element of phrasing — "the expressive grouping of musical sounds," as Hubert Foss has defined it.

For instance, in the opening measures of the slow movement of the "Appassionata" Sonata, our immediate impression is the wonder of the first three chords (see the example on page 41): the Db major triad opening out, with the voices going in contrary motion to Gb, then closing in again to Db. Then the succeeding notes, where the melody is a reiterated Ab, and underneath are changing harmonies and a moving bass line.

The recognition of these two aspects of music — the movement of voices in relation to each other, and the harmonic changes under a held or repeated tone, are of great importance in phrasing.

Another example of the opening-out movement of harmonies is the beginning of Fauré's "Après un Rêve," where the melodic line of the song ascends against the two descending bass notes.

A familiar example of a reiterated tone in relation to changing harmonies is the Chopin "Raindrop" Prelude, Op. 28, No. 15. In the first and third sections of the piece, the Ab in the bass is a sort of reiterated organ point on which the music rests. In the middle section, Ab is enharmonically changed to G♯, and is now in the upper voice over changing harmonies in C♯ minor. The reiterated tone is continually changing its meaning with the succession of changing harmonies. The player should be sensitive to these subtle changes, and convey them in his performance.

Conclusion

Phrasing is, of course, enhanced by the inflection of the tones and by delicate nuances of dynamics. Here again, familiarity with the sound of music and general intelligence are our only guides. As we know, many of the marks of expression printed in music are incorrect or more frequently inadequate.

As a matter of fact, we do not make phrasing, we discover it. Even the markings are only the report of discoveries of what is inherent in the music. For example, we do not play a passage with a crescendo because the passage is so marked. It is marked crescendo because its own inherent meaning demands that it shall be played with an increase of tone. We do not retard at the end of a passage because the word "ritardando" is printed in the music. Here also, if the music is itself slowing up, the word is printed as a suggestion, perhaps only a reminder, of what the music itself implies.

We can say that a fine composition is beautifully phrased if the player conveys not only the rhythmic grouping, but all the nuances of meaning that are inherent in the music. Unless the listener is a trained musician, he may not be consciously aware of these details of the performance, but in any event, he will acquiesce with the music as it is unfolding. He will listen effortlessly, and will probably think that the music is beautiful.

On the other hand, if the phrases are run together, or if the performer himself is not aware of the melodic structure, or is not himself moved by the interplay of harmony and melody, the listener may not be aware that the piece is being badly played, but may think that it is a dull and uninteresting piece, which it is not!

There is no possible way of indicating in print all the subtleties of musical phrasing, any more than it would be possible to print an edition of Keats that would convey exactly the speed and stress and inflection that he himself would use in repeating, for example, the line:

"A thing of beauty is a joy forever."

When all is said and done, it is not the marks on the page that we follow in phrasing a musical passage. It is our musical knowledge and experience, our musical instinct, and eventually, our musical intuition that are the only guides that we can follow.

COUNTING

How very much of our search for knowledge involves Counting!

We try to harness Time itself by counting. We arrange calendars so that we may count years, months, weeks, and days. And we invent clocks and watches which will compute for us hours, and minutes, and seconds.

We measure Space in terms of numbers. Nowadays many a small boy considers the space ship a quite feasible means of locomotion between the Earth and the other heavenly bodies. He can tell you, for example, in terms of counting, the distance between here and the Moon, which he plans to visit. And again, using numbers, he can tell you how many hours are needed for the return trip.

The doctor, in making his diagnosis of our bodily condition, records his findings in terms of numbers. What is our pulse rate? How many times a minute do we breathe? What is the rate of our basic metabolism? What is our blood count?

We are always measuring, always reckoning, always counting.

But numbers serve other purposes besides such matters as recording with mathematical accuracy Time and Space and bodily health. The poet often uses numbers, which are not to be taken literally, but to be conceived imaginatively, to convey a sense of largeness. For example, Christopher Marlowe, invoking the vision of "Sweet Helen of Troy," exclaims, "Was this the face that launched a thousand ships?" And Wordsworth, with exuberant hyperbole, remembering a field of golden daffodils, says,

> Ten thousand saw I at a glance
> Tossing their heads in sprightly dance.

St. John in "The Revelation" writes,

> And they sung a new song . . .
> And I heard the voice of many angels round about the throne;
> and the number of them was thousands of thousands.

Numbers have symbolic meaning in the stupendous imagery of "The Revelation," as in the description of the

Dragon with seven heads, and ten horns,
And seven diadems upon his heads.

Counting occurs in many passages of the Bible. In Genesis we read
the story of the Seven Days of Creation. The fourth book of Moses is
itself called The Book of Numbers. In Saint Matthew we are told that
"the very hairs of your head are all numbered."

COUNTING AS IT RELATES TO MUSIC

What do we count in music? Primarily rhythmic units, that is,
patterns of pulsation. The reason for counting is not merely to recite
the number of beats in each measure, but to release the rhythmic feeling
of the music that is being performed.

The conductor's beat is a glorified sort of counting. Besides giving
the metrical patterns and rhythmic flow of the composition, the conductor is also conveying to the men in the orchestra by his beat the
speed, the phrasing, the inflection, and his interpretation of the emotional
content of the music that they are playing.

In discussing the subject of counting, the relationship of the details to
the whole must be considered. It makes a great difference, for instance,
if we think of small units first and then add them together to form large
ones, or if we think of a large unit first and then think of the small ones
of which it is composed. For example, there is a difference between
thinking that four sixteenth notes make a quarter, or that a quarter
beat is "embellished" by four sixteenth notes. Do we think that innumerable stars decorate the sky at midnight, or that the infinite heaven
is studded with stars? Browning said, "Image the whole, then execute
the parts."

The consideration of this point of view has a direct bearing
on counting as it relates to music. We can consider a symphony
as a whole musical concept. We can count the number of movements,
usually four. Then we can study the first movement, and can count
the large sections: frequently an introduction, then the exposition,
development, and recapitulation, and perhaps a coda. After that we
can count smaller sections, identifying the themes. We can count
the phrase lengths within each of these themes. Then, continuing
the process of focusing our attention on smaller and smaller details,
we can count the number of measures in the phrases, then the
number and arrangement of beats in each measure, and finally, perhaps, consider the number and arrangement of notes in each beat.

During this process our attention will have been funnelled down steadily from the conception of a symphony as a whole to, perhaps, the fraction of a pulse with which it begins. For example, Beethoven's Fifth Symphony is usually performed in half an hour. The first printed time value is an 8th rest!

Counting "By the Measure"

For years children have been told to count aloud while they practice. In the past, however, counting was usually a sing-song recitation of the beats in each measure from barline to barline, regardless of the rhythmic grouping of the notes. It was merely a statement of arithmetical verity.

I remember this vividly because my own early experiences with counting were very trying. When I began to read music and play duets with my sister, the book we used was Löw's "Teacher and Pupil." The first piece was a duet, in which I, as the pupil, played a succession of whole notes with the hands an octave apart. Underneath each note was printed "1 2 3 4," and this I had to recite aloud over and over while I played. It was very boring.

Later the teacher with whom I studied gave me Schumann's "Soldiers' March" to play, and with her, counting became fantastic! She insisted that while I played I count aloud what sounded to me like a strange chant: "One-an-duh, two-and, One-and, two-and, etc." She told me that in every piece the notes between the barlines belonged together. I began at each barline with the count "One," and took a breath before the next barline. I remember so well when she gave me an arrangement of Brahms's "Lullaby and Goodnight" to learn by myself. The piece is in 3 meter, and begins on the
4
third beat. She told me to be sure and count "One-and Two-and Three-and" for each measure, but to begin with "Three-and."

On reading the piece at home I was surprised to find that when it came to the last measure there was only a half note. I knew that if I were to count as directed, this probable mistake of the printer should be rectified, so I added a dot after the last half note in order to complete the measure and make it look tidy!

At the following lesson my teacher told me to rub out the dot, because this was an "incomplete measure of two beats." I asked her where the rest of the measure was, and she said, "at the beginning of the piece." So I tried playing the last note, counting "One-and

Two-and," and then playing the first notes of the piece, counting "Three-and." But this, of course, sounded absurd. My teacher said, "I didn't mean that you really play it that way! Incomplete measures *are* difficult, and you'll understand them when you're a little older."

Needless to say, this was many years ago. The teacher herself had no conception of counting in terms of rhythmic design, and it was not until much later that I discovered that there is no such thing as an "incomplete measure," that music is not usually grouped from barline to barline, and that this particular piece is counted "Three-*One*-Two."

RHYTHMIC DESIGN

The essential structural element in music is Rhythm. Rhythm means motion. In music, this motion expresses itself in recurrent patterns, usually consisting of one heavy beat, and one or more light beats. The arrangement of these beats is called Rhythmic Design. These designs are counted in various ways, depending on the position of the heavy beat in relation to the light beat or beats.

The barline is placed before the heavy beat of the pattern. This beat is affirmative, and is counted "One." The meter sign tells the number of beats between the barlines, but it does not tell the Rhythmic Design, that is, it does not tell the rhythmic grouping of the heavy and light beats.

In 2/4 meter there are two beats, one heavy and one light. Each beat is a quarter. Rhythmically either one can come first, so two rhythmic designs are possible. They would be counted either:

$$One\text{-Two} \qquad \text{or} \qquad Two\text{-}One$$

Quick pieces in 6/8 meter also have two beats in the measure, and are counted either "*One*-Two" or "Two-*One*," each unit here being a dotted quarter.

The English folksong "London Bridge is Falling Down" is in 2/4 meter. It begins on the first beat of the measure, and the tune is counted "*One*-Two." The French folksong, "Savez-vous planter les choux?" is in 6/8 meter. It begins on the second beat of the measure, and this tune is counted "Two-*One*."

Words themselves illustrate rhythmic design, and there is an interesting analogy between the rhythm of words and the rhythmic designs of music. For example, in almost all English words of two syllables one syllable is stressed more than the other. The word "Music" illustrates the stressed syllable coming first, so the rhythmic design of this word is "*One*-Two." The word "Delight" illustrates the light syllable coming first, so the rhythmic design of this word is "Two-*One*."

In 3 meter there are three beats, one heavy and two lighter ones,
4
so three rhythmic groupings are possible. They would be counted:

One-Two-Three   Three-*One*-Two   and Two-Three-*One*

depending upon the position of the heavy beat.

The Minuet from "Don Giovanni" is in 3 meter, and is an
4
example of the rhythmic design "*One*-Two-Three." "The Star-Spangled Banner," also in 3 meter, begins on the third beat, and
4
is counted "Three-*One*-Two." The comparatively rare rhythmic design "Two-Three-*One*" is illustrated by the beginning of the Beethoven-Kreisler "Rondino."

The words "Symphony," "Tchaikovsky," and "Clarinet" illustrate these three rhythmic designs, as in each word the stressed syllable comes in a relatively different place. "Symphony" would be counted "*One*-Two-Three"; "Tchaikovsky" would be counted "Three-*One*-Two"; "Clarinet" would be counted, "Two-Three-*One*".

Similarly, in 4 meter there are four rhythmic designs: "*One*-
4
Two-Three-Four," "Four-*One*-Two-Three," "Three-Four-*One*-Two," and "Two-Three-Four-*One*."

"Swanee River," "Auld Lang Syne," and the Gavotte from "Mignon" are well-known tunes that illustrate respectively the counts "*One*-Two-Three-Four," "Four-*One*-Two-Three," and "Three-Four-*One*-Two." I know of no tune in the rhythmic design "Two-Three Four-*One*" that is sufficiently well known to use as illustration.

The words "Modulating," "Harmonious," "Contrapuntal," and "Recitative" illustrate these four rhythmic designs. In each word the stressed syllable comes in a relatively different place rhythmically.

The same rhythmic designs are possible if the unit of the beat is a half note or an eighth note. For example,

would all be counted "Three-*One*-Two," the difference being in the speed of the beats.

Slow pieces in $\frac{6}{8}$ meter are counted "*One*-Two-Three-*Four*-Five-Six" with a beat for each eighth note. The slow movement of Beethoven's Sonata, Op. 7, is counted this way.

RELATIVE LENGTH OF BEATS

How do we make Rhythmic Design clear to the ear of the listener? By a slight lengthening of the last beat in the design. This lengthening or slackening serves to delineate the Rhythmic Design so that the grouping is easily heard. The slackening probably will not occur at the end of every design, unless the phrase is only one measure long, but will probably occur at the end of the phrase. The last beat of a Rhythmic Design is thus likely to be slightly longer than the other beats.

An excellent way to realize this relative length of beats is to make the basic motions that a conductor uses in "beating time." Holding a pencil lightly in your right hand, move your arm down and up in a straight line, as though conducting the Rhythmic Design "*One*-Two."

Repeat the motion several times at the same speed, saying first the direction, "Down-Up, Down-Up," and then the count, "*One*-Two, *One*-Two." Notice that you are instinctively slackening the motion of your arm at the end of the design, "Two," and that you are taking a "catch breath" after the count "Two."

Now reverse the order of the counts, and move your arm up and down as though conducting the Rhythmic Design "Two-*One*," saying, as you do so, first the direction, "Up-Down, Up-Down," and then the count, "Two-*One*, Two-*One*." In this case you will notice that your arm is instinctively slackening the motion on count "One," now the end of the design, and you will be taking a "catch breath" after the count "One."

When there are three beats in a measure, the conductor's arm follows the direction "Down" for count One, "Out" for count Two, and "Up" for count Three. The design can commence on any one of these three beats, but in each case you will find that the last count of the design is slightly longer than the others.

Similarly, in 4 meter, the arm moves in the directions "Down"
            4
for count One, "In" (across the body) for count Two, "Out" for count Three, and "Up" for count Four. There are four possible Rhythmic Designs, and in each the arm will instinctively slacken the motion on the last beat.

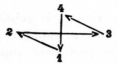

The recognition of Rhythmic Design is of the greatest importance, particularly in ensemble playing. If, for example, two children are playing as a duet a waltz with the Rhythmic Design "Three-*One*-Two," and the child playing the bass is counting "*One*-Two-Three," he will instinctively be lengthening count Three. If the child in the treble is counting "Three-*One*-Two," he will instinctively be lengthening count Two. The result can only be rhythmic confusion. It will be much better if both children, before they begin to play, realize that the Rhythmic Design of the piece is "Three-*One*-Two," and count softly together two measures, saying "Three-*One*-Two, Three-*One*-Two" before beginning to play. Thus they will start together, and the piece will be played rhythmically. So often the tendency is to begin counting with "One." Then the real rhythm is not established until after the piece is sounding, and it should be established before the piece begins.

If a conductor leading "The Star-Spangled Banner," for example, begins with a downbeat "One," and expects the chorus to come in on "Three," the rhythm of their performance at the beginning will be unsteady, since by starting on count "One," he has implied that count "Three" is going to be the longest. The tune, of course, is built on the Rhythmic Design "Three-*One*-Two," so throughout, count "Two"—the last beat of the phrase—is slightly longer than the other beats. If the conductor should start by beating a preliminary measure of "Three-*One*-Two," the performers would come in on an established rhythm, and there would be no rhythmic confusion.

Rhythmic design may change during the course of a piece. The first phrase may begin on count "One," and the following phrases begin on a light beat. It is important that the student be aware of the Rhythmic Design or Designs in the music he is playing, because this awareness is intimately connected with the phrasing.

DIFFERENT WAYS OF COUNTING THE SAME PASSAGE

Much music can be counted in several different ways, each of which will give a different rhythmic impression. Here, for example, are three ways in which many passages can be counted:

1. *Beats in each measure.* When a student first studies a piece, he will probably begin by counting the beats in each measure, in order to be sure that he is playing the time-values correctly.

2. *Beats in each phrase.* In order to have a better understanding of the phrase lengths, he can count the beats in each phrase, irrespective of the barlines. The speed of the beats will be the same as in the first version.

3. *Measures in each phrase.* Here the musical effect will be very different from either of the other two versions, since in counting the measures in the phrase, the counts are now slower. The player identifies whole measures instead of single beats, although, of course, the notes are played at the same speed as before.

The following passage illustrates these three ways of counting:

1.) Beats in each measure:	1	2	3	1	2	3	1 2	3
2.) Beats in the phrase:	1	2	3	4	5	6	7 8	9
3.) Measures in the phrase:	1			2			3	

1. Counting the beats in each measure: "*One*-Two-Three, *One*-Two-Three, *One*-Two-Three." This version stresses the meter, and though arithmetically correct, gives no sense of the long line of the phrase.

2.   Counting the beats in the phrase: "*One*-Two-Three-Four-Five-Six-Seven-Eight-Nine." This version is quieter. Though the beats are of the same speed as above, the musical effect is of a longer line, because we feel only one downbeat.

3.   Counting the measures in the phrase: "*One*—Two—Three—." Each count represents a whole measure, so each count is three times as slow as in the other two versions. This last way of counting gives a still calmer rhythmic feeling, because of the slower speed of the count, though the notes, of course, are still played at the same speed.

Many passages can be counted in these three ways, many cannot. Questions of phrases beginning on a weak beat have to be considered. But you will often find that passages that sound hurried and "notey" when the metrical beats are stressed will be played with much greater ease and fluency if longer units, such as complete measures, are felt. This is true of pieces as different in character as Heller's "Avalanche," the Schumann "Romanza" in F-sharp, the Beethoven Sonata in C minor, Op. 10, No. 1, the first movement of the Schumann Piano Concerto, and most Chopin waltzes.

The last movement of the Beethoven Sonata, Op. 31, No. 2, is written with the meter sign $\frac{3}{8}$. Most of the phrases are four measures long, and if the player counts the *measures* in the phrase rather than the *beats* in each measure, the piece will sound convincing and be far easier to play. "The Blue Danube" flows along comfortably at the beginning if *measures* are counted in the pattern of "Four-*One*-Two-Three." Later the phrasing of the measures changes.

There are innumerable instances where the number of beats given in a meter sign does not indicate the Rhythmic Design that the composer obviously intended. For example, many of the slow movements of early sonatas are marked $\frac{2}{4}$, where the obvious meaning of the music is four beats to the measure, and the meter sign might be $\frac{4}{8}$.

In general we may say that the impression of the speed of a performance depends upon the speed of the *beats* rather than the speed of the *notes*.

PLAN OF COUNT

To insure that a student is aware of the phrase lengths and their organization in the pieces he is studying, it is a good idea for him

to write out a Plan of Count of the piece, arranging the number
of beats in each phrase on a line. Music, of course, is usually printed
in solid block-like form that *looks* like prose. But because of its
rhythmic life, much music *sounds* like poetry. Writing the number
of counts in each phrase on a separate line makes a piece look
like poetry, and gives a clear idea of the piece as a whole, and a
sure feeling of the relationship of the different phrases.

```
3        ⎡ 3 │ 1  2  3 │ 1  2
4        ⎢ 3 │ 1  2
         ⎣ 3 │ 1  2

         ⎡ 3 │ 1  2  3 │ 1  2
         ⎣ 3 │ 1  2  3 │ 1  2    etc.
```

Notice the "rhyming" scheme of the phrase lengths: 2 measures,
balanced by 1 measure plus 1 measure. Then 2 measures balanced
by 2 more measures.

Here is the Plan of Count of the Brahms Waltz in A-flat:

```
3              │ 1  2
4
        ♪ 3    │ 1  2

        ♪ 3 │ 1  2  3 │ 1  2    etc.
```

Hear the buildup at the end of each line to the A♭ triad with C in
the soprano.

The Plan of Count of Mendelssohn's "Consolation" could be
written as follows:

```
4          3  4 │ 1  2
4      ♪ 3  4 │ 1  2
           3  4 │ 1  2
       ♪ 3  4 │ 1  2
```

Notice that the prevailing count is 3 4 | 1 2. The first and
third lines begin directly on count "Three," the second and fourth
begin with a preliminary eighth note. In reciting this, say the word
"eighth" or perhaps the sound "Oo" for the eighth note.

Another familiar piece that lends itself easily to what we may call "structural counting" is Grieg's "Butterfly." The piece is in $\frac{4}{4}$ meter, and the counts are all quarters. The piece can be played with rhythmic understanding if it is counted in normal phrase lengths, though this necessitates disregarding sometimes the metrical barlines.

mm. 1-2
```
⎡1  2  3  4
⎢1  2
⎣1  2
```

mm. 3-6
```
⎡1  2  3  4
⎢1  2  3  4
⎣1  2  3  4  5  6  7  8   :‖
```

mm. 7-8   ‖:
(mm. 24-25)
```
⎡1  2  3  4
⎢1  2
⎣1  2
```

mm. 9-10
(mm. 26-27)
```
[1  2  3  4  5  6  7  8
```

mm. 11-12
(mm. 28-29)
```
⎡1  2  3  4
⎢1  2
⎣1  2
```

mm. 13-16
(mm. 30-33)
```
⎡1  2  3  4
⎢1  2  3  4
⎢1  2
⎢1  2
⎢1  2
⎣1  2
```

mm. 17-18
(mm. 34-35)
```
⎡1  2  3  4
⎢1  2
⎣1  2
```

mm. 19-23
(mm. 36-40)
```
⎡1  2  3  4
⎢1  2  3  4
⎢1  2  3  4
⎣1  2  3  4  5  6  7  8   :‖
```

(mm. 41-42)
```
[1  2  3  4  5  6  7  8
```

One young pianist played for me the Chopin "Black Key" Etude in a pedestrian fashion. She was accustomed to counting the piece throughout "*One*-Two," and her playing, though facile, was rhythmically very rigid. I suggested that she investigate the harmonic structure and the phrase lengths of the piece, and then experiment with counting different time values: eighths, or quarters, or halves.

Eventually she worked out an ingenious Plan of Count for the Etude. The piece is printed in 2/4 meter. Sometimes she counted four eighths to a measure, sometimes the number of quarter beats in a phrase, and sometimes she counted the number of measures in an entire passage, counting only the half notes as the harmonies changed. Her Plan of Count, suggested by the music itself, began as follows:

4/8	♪ ♪ ♪ ♪ 1 2 3 4	m. 1
	♪ ♪ ♪ ♪ 1 2 3 4	m. 2
2/4	♩ ♩ 1 2	m. 3
	♩ ♩ 1 2	m. 4
4/8	♪ ♪ ♪ ♪ 1 2 3 4	m. 5
	♪ ♪ ♪ ♪ 1 2 3 4	m. 6
2/4	♩ ♩ ♩ ♩ 1 2 3 4	mm. 7-8

(Measures 9 through 16 are a repetition of measures 1-8.)

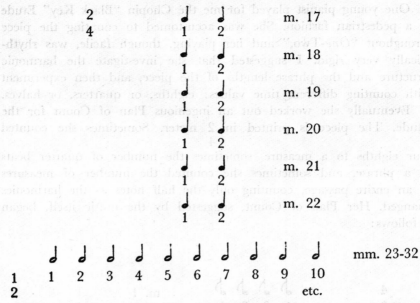

She worked out her Plan of Count for the rest of the Etude in the same fashion, and was able to play the composition with much more rhythmic vitality than when she was following the metrical count of two quarters for each measure. Many other arrangements of counting the "Black Key" Etude are possible, but the one quoted here gives a sense of the flexible over-all line of the phrasing.

DOES A PHRASE BEGIN WITH A REST?

Does any piece of music begin with silence? Does any piece really begin with a rest? This question of the notation of the first measure of a piece is intriguing. Here are the beginnings of several pieces:

But the Bach F major Invention is usually printed $\frac{3}{4}$ 𝅘𝅥𝅮 𝅘𝅥𝅮𝅘𝅥𝅮 𝅘𝅥𝅮𝅘𝅥𝅮 𝅘𝅥 | 𝅘𝅥𝅮

instead of $\frac{3}{4}$ 𝅘𝅥𝅮 𝅘𝅥𝅮𝅘𝅥𝅮 𝅘𝅥𝅮𝅘𝅥𝅮 𝅘𝅥 | 𝅘𝅥𝅮 . This last gives a clear picture of the

phrase heading for the count "One," and not beginning with a superfluous first beat of silence. Similarly, why not print the beginning

of the C major Invention $\frac{4}{4}$ 𝅘𝅥𝅮𝅘𝅥𝅮𝅘𝅥𝅮 𝅘𝅥𝅮𝅘𝅥𝅮𝅘𝅥𝅮𝅘𝅥𝅮 𝅘𝅥𝅮𝅘𝅥𝅮 𝅘𝅥𝅮𝅘𝅥𝅮 | 𝅘𝅥𝅮 instead of

$\frac{4}{4}$ 𝄾 𝅘𝅥𝅮𝅘𝅥𝅮𝅘𝅥𝅮 𝅘𝅥𝅮𝅘𝅥𝅮𝅘𝅥𝅮𝅘𝅥𝅮 𝅘𝅥𝅮𝅘𝅥𝅮 𝅘𝅥𝅮𝅘𝅥𝅮 | 𝅘𝅥𝅮 ?

One classic example of a composition beginning with a rest has always puzzled me. It is the opening of the Beethoven Fifth Symphony. When we think of the first measures or sing the melody, we certainly do not feel a downbeat until we get to the long E♭. I suppose it is humanly impossible for a conductor to hypnotize an orchestra into beginning the first measure playing the three preliminary G's together without benefit of a preliminary downbeat. But the whish of the conductor's descending baton on the first 8th rest always seems to me a rhythmic contradiction. It starts the first figure off with two downbeats, one at the beginning, and one at the end. All of the first part of the movement is, of course, a development of the rhythmic figure of three light notes pushing toward a heavy one. There are not many words in English that fit the rhythmic grouping, but one of them is "Superimpose." I have often wished that this superfluous downbeat were not "superimposed" at the beginning of this Titanic movement!

CONCLUSION

This chapter has discussed in some detail ways of studying a composition rhythmically. The whole purpose of counting is that we may be aware of the vital energy that flows in patterns through any composition, from the smallest melody to the greatest symphony.

EAR TRAINING

"Isn't ear training the most important thing we have to discuss?" exclaimed a young enthusiast at a meeting of piano teachers. "If we don't play by ear, what in heaven's name do we play by?" It was a refreshing breeze and lightened the serious atmosphere of the meeting, where teaching sight reading, memorizing, technique, and other subjects had been discussed. A lively exchange of views followed as to the place of ear training in the piano student's education.

In many places, such as the admirable High School of Music and Art in New York City, applicants for admission take exhaustive tests in ear training in order that their response to sound may be evaluated. Ear training tests of various kinds, if given periodically, can record the student's progress in hearing such fundamentals of music as pitch, rhythm, intensity or acuity of sound, and so on. But these tests have to do only with what the physical ear hears. In listening to music, however, the mind, the emotions, and the imagination are also engaged.

Many students have an idea, because they have so-called perfect pitch, that their ears are trained. I have heard it stated that one person in about two hundred has this peculiar ability to identify by name certain pitches. This is a kind of auditory memory that has nothing to do with music, except for the fact that sound is involved.

Many musicians have perfect pitch, and many have not. If a person has so discriminating a color sense that he can distinguish many different shades of red, he is not necessarily an artist. A music student who has perfect pitch is not necessarily a musician. A sense of relative pitch, however, can be acquired in varying degrees by anyone, and puts him on the road to being a musician.

So, the piano teacher's task is to see to it first that the student *hears* every sound that he makes, and second that his knowledge of music is constantly enlarging so that he *understands* what he hears.

LISTENING TO MUSICAL STRUCTURE

Listening to music can be more than relaxing into a bath of pleasant or exciting sensations. Recognition of design in a composition, and of its realization by the performer, can be a source of great pleasure.

In studying the pieces he is playing, or in listening to other music, the student's ear must always be alert. Obviously, the more he knows of music the more he will hear, and the greater will be his enjoyment. For example, if he has felt and understood in the pieces that he has studied, the dramatic tension of suspension, or the surprise of the deceptive cadence, or the ambiguity of the diminished seventh chord, or the comfortable finality of the plagal cadence, he will be able to recognize them if they occur in music that he is listening to, and his emotional response to the music will be greater.

I do not mean that in attending a concert his attention should be focused on spotting these details of composition to the exclusion of his enjoyment of the music as a whole. But it would be a pity if, in listening to music, he received only an emotional impression without at the same time recognizing something of the technical skill that has been employed both in the writing and in the performing of the music.

When we go to the circus and the lady in pink tights swings from her high trapeze, and the gentleman in blue tights leaves his trapeze at the calculated fraction of a second necessary to catch her in mid-air, we are emotionally thrilled by their intrepidity and the rhythmic beauty of their performance. But we also admire the technique, the hours of bodily discipline that have gone into perfecting the act.

EAR TRAINING FOR CHILDREN

In his earliest years the child's contact with music is, of course, through his ears. His mother sings him to sleep. In the kindergarten he dances and marches to music. He learns little songs by imitation, and perhaps makes up songs of his own. His teacher claps rhythmic phrases which he repeats or answers. He plays singing games, dramatizing the text. He is constantly coordinating what he hears with what he does.

Making Aural Comparisons

A small girl was learning to play triads, and I thought that she could discover by ear the function of the damper pedal. So I asked her to play the chord F A C and to listen to the sound. Then I asked her to press down the damper pedal, and to play the chord again, and see if there was any difference in the sound.

She pressed her foot on the pedal, played the chord, and beamed as she said with lovely alliteration: "It makes more music"!

Much more that goes into a piano lesson than is generally supposed can first be presented to the young student through his ear. For example, suppose you are going to teach him two of the Italian terms used in music to indicate speed. If you are teaching him the difference between Allegro and Andante, you should not begin by showing him these words in his music book and explaining what they mean. Rather, you will play a short phrase first quickly, then more slowly, asking him to listen. Then you will ask him to describe the difference between the two. He will probably say one was fast and the other was slow. Then you can tell him that most musical directions are written in Italian, and that the Italian word for going quickly is Allegro, and for going slowly is Andante, and finally show him these words in his book. Thus aural comparisons made and described by the child have been the basis of learning these terms. He has used his ears, his mind, and, last of all, his eyes.

You can use the same procedure in teaching him the terms *forte* and *piano*. Play a short phrase, first loudly and then softly, and ask him to tell you the difference. Then supply the Italian words *forte* and *piano* with their abbreviations *f* and *p*, and show him an example of these markings in his book.

One little boy I taught had difficulty in remembering which is which, until I got him to say in a whisper "*p* stands for *piano* and means soft," and to shout "*f* stands for *forte* and means loud." I also told him that the piano's complete name is pianoforte, and that you can play both soft and loud on it.

If a child is to make these aural comparisons, be careful that in your playing you make only one difference at a time. For example, the following two-measure phrases differ in four ways:

1. Mode. (The first phrase is major, the second is minor.)
2. Touch. (Staccato and Legato.)
3. Speed. (The time values in the second phrase are twice as long as those in the first.)
4. Dynamics. (The first is *forte,* the second *piano*.)

If you play the two phrases as printed above, and ask the child what is the difference between the two, his ear may be quite confused. But if you begin by playing the first phrase as written, and then repeat the same phrase in minor, without changing the touch or speed or dynamics, there will be only one change for him to report on. Then you might again play the first phrase as written, and repeat it *piano*, without changing the mode or the touch or the speed. And so on.

Later, as his hearing and power of aural analysis develop, you might play an example like the two phrases given above, tell him that there are four points of difference between them, and ask him if he can hear and describe all four.

Playing by Ear

Playing by ear is viewed with suspicion by many parents as well as teachers. How often a gifted child will be happily engaged in investigating music at the piano trying to pick out a familiar tune, only to be thwarted by his mother's voice from the next room saying: "That's not practicing. Get out your books and practice your lesson." She feels that if he plays by ear he will, perhaps, never learn to read.

But it seems to me that in early piano study, playing by ear, learning pieces by rote, and learning to read should all three proceed simultaneously. They are three different avenues that lead to the same goal, which is the performance of music. The child who plays by ear is probably one who later on will improvise easily and may, in time, compose. Such a child is a challenge to the teacher's ingenuity. He is obviously interested in making music and this, of course, is an asset and can be turned to good account in various ways. For example, it can lead to his developing a sense of fingering.

The teacher might suggest that the child play by ear a familiar tune such as "Swanee River," beginning with his right hand third finger on F♯. This, of course, will bring the tune in the key of D. The child may be asked to finger the tune carefully, making as few hand shifts as possible, so that the phrasing may be smooth. Thus he will discover that phrasing and fingering go together.

Or, if the teacher wishes to stress the rhythmic side of his playing, the child may be asked, while he plays the tune by ear, to count "*One-Two-Three-Four*" steadily. Or, perhaps while he plays he can sing the time values of the tune. It begins "Ha - alf — Two-eighths, Two-eighths, Quarter, Quarter, Two-eighths, Tie." Later, he may become interested in learning to *write* the melody that he has picked out by ear. In this way he will learn the necessity of writing down the correct notes and correct time values, so that someone else can play what he has written.

We must always keep in mind that we are teaching people whose varying capacities we discover and develop. We are not teaching music as a subject that must be learned conventionally by all students along the same rigid lines.

Teaching Technique by Ear

The object of technique is, of course, to produce tone. The child should learn very early in his studies that there are different ways of touching the keys, each of which will produce a different tone quality. For instance, if he plays C D E with fingertips touching the keys and using the weight of his arm to depress them, the tone will be entirely different than if he plays the same keys with a light arm and uses a high finger action. He should learn in his own playing how different tone qualities are produced, and should be able to recognize and reproduce these qualities when he hears other people play.

An excellent way to teach technique by ear is to use two pianos. The teacher plays short phrases or chords on one piano and the pupil tries not only to repeat the notes, but also to imitate the tone quality on the second piano. His ear will be quickened, and he will learn, for example, that a warm, singing tone cannot be reproduced if his arm is stiff or if his fingers are lifeless. Eventually, the technique he acquires and the resultant sounds he produces will be completely synchronized in his ear, his mind, and his body.

Identifying Rhythmic Design

You may wish to end a piano lesson on "Wings of Song," and to include some ear training of rhythmic design. In the last few minutes of the lesson play to the child several short pieces, each in a different meter and with different "counts." Have him sit beside you as you play, and tell him to "feel for the *Ones*," that is, to identify the down beats, by touching his knee lightly with his closed fist, and saying *"One"* as he does so. Then, while you continue playing, have him count aloud all the beats that he hears, still emphasizing the *"Ones."* He has now discovered the meter of the piece. And finally, have him discover the order of the beats in the rhythmic design.

Here is the report of such a procedure written by an eight-year-old second-year pupil in his notebook:

Listener's Program — Rhythmic Design

1. Schubert — Military March — Count | 1 2
2. Wagner — Pilgrims' Chorus — Count 3 | 1 2
3. Old Black Joe — Count | 1 2 3 4
4. Annie Laurie — Count 4 | 1 2 3

The spelling of some of the words was dictated, but the whole procedure took less than ten minutes.

This training in recognizing rhythmic design is valuable in strengthening a child's sense of phrasing.

A CLASS OF TEEN-AGERS LISTENS TO THE FIRST MOVEMENT OF A SONATA

This is a short account of a lesson in ear training given to a group of boys and girls twelve and thirteen years old. They had been studying music for four years, during which time they had had piano lessons and had attended a weekly class in musicianship. The teacher was an experienced and very resourceful young woman.

As we approached the classroom, pandemonium seemed to be going on inside. When we opened the door the noise ceased suddenly. It felt like that moment of grateful hush before an orchestral concert, when the players stop warming up and cease practicing scales and hard bits of the program, because the oboe-player has risen and is about to "give the A."

Two boys were seated at the piano. Miss W............. inquired what they had been playing, and they said cheerfully "Oh, we were improvising boogie-woogie introducing the Augmented Sixth Chord."

Miss W............. said she was sorry to interrupt the flow of genius, but that the class was about to have an informal test in ear training. She said that she was going to play a piece they had not studied, and first they were to make a list of some of the things they might expect to hear and recognize in the composition.

She went to the blackboard and asked the children to dictate a list. Hands shot up all over the room, and soon there was a formidable list of nearly thirty items that they had dictated. The list began:

Meter
Count
Speed words (Allegro, Andante, etc.)
Mode (major or minor)
Style (harmonic or contrapuntal)

Scale tunes or chord tunes
Non-harmonic tones, such as
  Passing notes
  Suspensions
  Appoggiaturas
  Changing Notes
Form, such as
  A-B-A
  Variation
  Rondo
Cadences, such as
  Authentic
  Plagal
  Deceptive
Unusual Chords, such as
  Augmented Sixth
  Repetitions
  Sequences
  Motions
    Parallel
    Contrary
    Oblique
  Dynamics

All of these had been presented to the children first by ear, and the terms, which they used so freely, were the identification of familiar musical experiences.

Then Miss W............. played the first movement of a Mozart sonata with which the class was unfamiliar. At the conclusion the children eagerly reported some of the points of interest that they had noticed.

After that Miss W............. played the movement again, phrase by phrase, and the children wrote in their notebooks a running description of the music. Some, of course, heard more than others, but all of them were aware that music was something that they could listen to with interest and could discuss intelligently.

This lesson reminded me of a class of teen-agers that I was teaching which one day was visited by the Russian pianist Ossip Gabrilowitsch. He said that he could stay only fifteen minutes. The children sang and played pieces, and he seemed interested. But he stayed on and on. At the end of a half hour I resorted to ear training. I played chords that the children had studied, and asked the class to identify them by name. All went well until I played a Neapolitan Sixth. There was silence, until a little boy said, "I can play it, and I know where it goes, but I forget the name."

From the back of the room came the voice of Mr. Gabrilowitsch: "Children: Think of ice cream!" The youngsters said in chorus, "Neapolitan Sixth!" and the session ended on a note of hilarity.

TEACHING SONGS BY EAR TO A CLASS OF ADULTS

In addition to the regular curriculum for class work in musicianship, including harmony, theory, and analysis, one of the most rewarding experiences for a class of adults is learning to sing by ear a repertory of fine songs.

Adults are so accustomed to learning through the eye that the experience of learning through the ear is novel and usually intriguing to them. At first they may lack confidence in their ability to learn by ear, but it is astonishing how quickly they will learn to trust their musical intuition.

Most of us, in listening to music, are unconsciously "hearing ahead" and anticipating what we think will come next. You can prove this to a class by playing, for instance, the chord C D F♯, and asking the group to sing the F♯. Then ask them to "hear ahead" and sing what note they think will come next, and they will probably sing G, because they have heard the familiar idiom of a dominant seventh resolving to a tonic hundreds of times. Or play the chord C E♭ B♭, and ask them to "hear ahead" and sing the tone to which B♭ will probably move. They will probably sing A♭, or perhaps A. In these two examples, it is the harmony that is influencing the movement of the tones.

You can also demonstrate to a class their ability intuitively to hear ahead by playing a short melodic pattern on the first scale step, and then repeating it on the second scale step. Ask them to sing what you have played, and to continue singing what might come next. They will probably continue to sing the pattern in sequence up the entire scale, because sequential progressions up and down the scale are a familiar idiom in a great deal of music that they have heard. Eventually, if you improvise short phrases or complete melodies, the class will sing, following the tune, much as a congregation in church will follow an unfamiliar hymn tune.

It is this innate musical intuition that can be relied on in teaching a class to learn songs by ear.

During the first eight weeks of a course in musicianship for adults that I once conducted, the students learned to sing by ear the melodies of the following songs:

1. "Für Musik" — Robert Franz
2. "Ein Ton" — Peter Cornelius
3. "The First Primrose" — Grieg
4. "Die Lotosblume" — Schumann
5. "Träume" — Wagner
6. "Up, Up, My Heart, With Gladness" — Bach
7. "Après un Rêve" — Fauré
8. "Traum durch die Dämmerung" — Richard Strauss

These songs were chosen primarily because they are beautiful, but also because each song illustrated some of the points of musical structure that we were discussing in the lessons.

We spent about ten minutes at the beginning of each session learning a song by ear. At the end of eight weeks the class sang in succession the eight songs that they had learned. Without interruption, I modulated from one song to the next. As soon as they heard the opening notes of each song, they "picked up" the melody and without any spoken direction from me, they began singing as though they were greeting familiar friends, which indeed they were. I felt that no matter what the students might have learned in the class *about* music, through singing these songs they had had a vital experience of *making* music which they would always remember.

It may be interesting to a teacher who has never taught songs in this way to describe in detail how one of these songs was learned. For instance, "Für Musik" by Robert Franz was an easy song to learn, because of the sequential construction and the obvious cadences.

First I spoke very briefly about the composer and the meaning of the poem and the circumstances under which the song was written. Then I played the song straight through in the key of D-flat, incorporating the vocal line in the accompaniment, so that the class could hear the song as a whole. Then, while I played, they sang by ear the first 2-measure phrase, which begins on D♭. They hummed or sang "Lah." (In learning a song by ear, it is better to have a class hum or sing "Lah," rather than having them learn the words, which may be in an unfamiliar language, or in an inadequate English translation. In singing a neutral syllable or humming, their attention will be focused on the melodic line, and they will have the experience of following the melodies as pure music.)

This first phrase of "Für Musik," beginning on D♭, is made of six notes, and the curve of the melody is in a small compass. I asked the class if they thought the last note of the phrase should be sung loud or soft, and they all agreed that it should be soft. (Later they would learn that this is the resolution of an appoggiatura.) The next phrase is a sequence of the first one, and begins on E♭. So, while I played this phrase, I asked the class to sing the same tune, beginning a tone higher than they had before.

The song continues with the same phrase, now beginning on G♭, and this they sang easily. Then I said that they had sung the phrase three times, each time at a higher pitch, and that now the melody blossomed out into an ascending broken chord, F A♭ D♭. I played this phrase, and they sang along with the piano, catching this idiomatic grouping of tones at once. The last tone of the upward curve, D♭, is held while the accompaniment plays three different chords. We spent a few moments talking about this detail. They sustained the high D♭, while listening to the changing harmonies beneath it, and realized that the "feeling" of the three chords was quite different, each being less dissonant than the previous one. They realized that these harmonic changes implied a diminuendo in the music, and that the "color" of the tone that they were singing was changing with each successive harmony. Then they sang in succession the four phrases they had learned. These phrases are the melody of the first and second stanzas of the song.

In the third and last stanza, the structure is similar, but the shape of the melodic figure is slightly altered. This new shape, which they caught quickly by ear, begins on D♭, and is repeated on E♭ and G♭, as in the first stanza.

The fourth phrase begins with a lovely upward sweep along the E♭ minor chord (G♭ B♭ E♭), which is a tone higher than the broken chord on D♭ in the corresponding phrase of the stanzas that they had already sung. The melody then turns and comes down the scale to A♭. They caught this curving phrase at once, following instinctively in their singing the natural crescendo and diminuendo of the curve as I played it. Then, to balance this high point of interest, the melody concludes with a most conventional and discreet cadence on the scale steps 1 3 2 1 — D♭ F E♭ D♭, and the song is ended.

Now they sang the song straight through. It had taken about ten minutes to learn it by ear. Following this, we went on to the class lesson. But at the end of the session, they sang "Für Musik" once more, in order to leave the room with music in their ears.

The class learned to sing the other songs following the same general procedure: First I played the song straight through, then spoke about it briefly, and then we studied it in detail. None of the class had had much musical instruction, and they were astonished to find how much repetition there is in many melodies. Through singing by ear and discussing the songs, they learned that music is full of idioms that they had heard many times. In other words, music was to them a more familiar language than they had realized. In being able to "hear ahead" what was coming, they were greatly cheered when they discovered that they did have some intuitive knowledge of music, and could rely on this intuition.

Here are some of the points that were discussed in the other songs the class learned by ear:

2) "Ein Ton" of Peter Cornelius is a beautiful example of the change of meaning of a tone when it is combined with different harmonies. The melody of this song is all on one tone, and it is surrounded by a wealth of wonderful moving harmonies that constantly change the character of that tone. The students were sensitive to the dynamics of the piano part as they sang, and reflected in their voices the changes of meaning of the tone itself because of the constantly changing harmonies.

3) "The First Primrose" of Grieg illustrates, among other things, an interesting contrast in the size and direction of intervals: in the first phrase the ascending sixth, followed immediately by the descending half step. It is a very easy song to learn by ear, since many of the phrases are immediately repeated, which is so characteristic of Grieg. (I illustrated this use of repetition by playing the beginnings of some other familiar pieces by this composer: "Morning" and "Ase's Death" from the "Peer Gynt" Suite, and some of the little piano pieces — "Berceuse," "Love Song," "To Spring" — and the first phrases of the Piano Concerto.) The middle part of "The First Primose" is charming. It is made of little ascending "curls" in whole and half steps, derived from the descending half step of the first phrase. While they sang, the class "pantomimed" the outline of the melody in the air. The last curl is down. Everybody waited on the last note of the last curl, until the harmony had pushed the music around to face the original key.

4) "Die Lotosblume" preceded a lesson on suspensions.

5) "Träume" was studied as an introduction to appoggiaturas.

6) "Up, Up, My Heart, With Gladness" is a forthright chorale melody, and was learned easily. The class noted the sequential construction and the pattern of contrasting phrase lengths: first two groups of 7 measures, then four 3-measure phrases.

7) "Après un Rêve," with the sinuous arabesques of the triplet figures, was studied when we were talking about melodic decoration.

8) In "Traum durch die Dämmerung" the class was particularly aware of the beautiful balance between the melody and the accompaniment and the lovely harmonies in the last phrase.

In every case the experience of singing the song came before the detailed analysis of the musical material.

There are many excellent collections of beautiful songs that can be learned by ear, and will greatly enlarge any student's experience of music. One of the books I use is called "50 Mastersongs," edited by Henry T. Finck and published by Oliver Ditson. It is advisable to get a collection where the songs are printed in a low key.

Sometimes *after* a class has learned a song by ear, you can give them all copies of the song and have them sing the melody, following the score, while you play the accompaniment. They will probably enjoy seeing the music that they have heard and sung.

Sometimes, in songs where the accompaniment has a life of its own quite independent of the vocal line, you can play the accompaniment on one piano, while a student at a second piano plays the vocal line with the left hand, duplicating it an octave higher with the right hand, so that the class can hear clearly the melody that they are following.

Singing songs by ear does not demand that one have a trained voice. This is not essential. What is essential is that the musical faculty be quickened, and that the memory be stored with as much great music as possible.

CONCLUSION

Some years ago, when traveling in Switzerland, I visited a school for deaf mutes. A very gifted teacher was working with a group of a dozen six- and seven-year-old children. The children sat in a circle in the gymnasium, and the teacher sat at a grand piano at one end of the room. She raised her arm and beckoned to them. They dashed across the room like bees to a pot of honey. Then she played a rhythmic chord-pattern over and over with a strong emphasis and very steady beats. The children touched any part of the piano that they could reach in order to feel the vibrations. Some children were on the floor under the piano, with ears pressed against the sounding board. Some were leaning against the legs and the sides of the piano, and one little boy climbed on a chair and touched the piano lid with his fingertips.

As soon as a child felt the vibration of the rhythmic pattern he would start off, marching around the room in time with it. When all the children had caught the rhythm and were marching in time, the teacher signalled again with her arm, and they ran back to their seats. They sat on the front edges of their chairs, ready to dash again to the piano when she signalled that she would play a new time-pattern. It was infinitely touching to see the joy in the little faces as the children responded to the vibrations that they could feel but could not hear.

The children also played games, rolling large balls rhythmically from one to another, and at the end of the lesson they left the room walking in pairs, keeping in time with each other.

The teacher, who was an excellent musician, told us that the children had a music class every day, and that it did wonders for their general development. Timid children became confident, boisterous ones quieted down. She said that their increasing sensitivity to vibrations helped in most cases in the process of learning to speak. She was a most inspiring and creative person.

Her work was a moving demonstration of the power of music, and especially the power of rhythm, to release some of the inner splendor of these handicapped little ones.

That summer I also visited a music school where a class of adults was having an ear training lesson. The teacher would sing a phrase, and the class would repeat it. The phrases became longer and more and more complicated as the lesson proceeded. At one point most of the students repeated the phrase incorrectly. The teacher stopped them and said gently: "Hören Sie in sich" (Hear within yourselves). Then he sang the phrase again. The class listened quietly for a moment, then the phrase was sung correctly by everyone.

Visiting these two schools strengthened my deep conviction that music resides in all of us. It is not something to be taught from without, but to be experienced from within. Developing this inner hearing is the aspect of music education that is called "Ear Training."

PRACTICING

As the piano student sits at the keyboard to practice, he has two objectives: to understand the music he is playing, and to train his fingers, hands, and arms. So practicing includes studying music as well as learning how to play it.

My aim in this chapter is to give some suggestions on how children and adults may make the best use of the time they spend practicing.

THE CHILD'S PRACTICE PERIOD

Ideally, the child should feel that the practice period is a time for investigation and discovery, and that studying music is much more entertaining, for instance, than learning a spelling lesson or doing sums in arithmetic. It is not in the same class with other things he does every day. Nor is he practicing to please his teacher, or to keep on friendly terms with his mother. He is engaged in the fascinating pursuit of finding out something about music. This is what happens to a child who is musically gifted, and who has a teacher who is also musically gifted!

But I believe that all children are potentially musical, and part of the teacher's business is to convince the child that practicing is not repetitious drudgery.

HOW TO PRACTICE
(This applies to older students as well as to children.)
Studying Before You Play

The more you study, the less you'll have to practice! This is true with students of all ages, from the child learning to play the German folk-tune "Ach, du lieber Augustin" to an older student learning a Beethoven sonata. By this I mean that the student should look over the whole piece, to get a clear idea of the structure, before beginning to practice the piece.

Frequently a piece is constructed with so much repetition that the discovery of this before he begins to play gives the pupil a pleasant feeling that it will really be easy to learn. "Ach, du lieber Augustin," for instance, is made of sixteen measures. But there are only four *different* measures. If a child looks over the music and discovers this encouraging fact before beginning to play the piece, he will think of it as an easy piece, as he realizes that there are only four different measures that he must learn to play.

Study before Practicing has been one of my theme songs for a long time. It was once the basis of a poem made by a class of students that I was teaching at the Mannes School. At the end of the term, the students of the school put on a show, poking fun at their teachers, and I came in for my share.

The poem, called "Diller's Darlings," was set to music by one of the students, and was sung vociferously by the entire class. This was the chorus:

> Will the children in this school
> Kindly follow the following rule:
> Do not practice when you study,
> Or you'll make your minds all muddy.
> But the really, truly fact is
> You must study when you practice!
> Will the children in this school
> Kindly follow this good rule?

Listening While You Play

The student of any age should constantly bear in mind, while practicing, that he is dealing with this wonderful art of Music, which is expressed in sound, and is to be *heard*. Our ears should always be active and we should listen with attention and interest to every sound we make.

Many times a student will play a passage and will realize at once that it did not sound as he expected. Often he will immediately play it over again in the same way, hoping that by virtue of repetition, it will turn out differently. Instead, after playing the passage the first time, he should quietly "listen back" in his mind to what he has just played, hear in his mind what he wishes to sound different, and decide how he is going to improve his performance. This time it will certainly sound different.

Singing While You Practice

I am a great believer, particularly with children, in having them sing while they practice. Singing is the most natural way of making music. Almost everyone in singing a melody will phrase it so that it makes sense. But we all know how unintelligently fingers can sometimes play the same melody so that it makes no sense at all. Therefore if a child sings, and plays while he sings, there is a good chance that his playing will be musically intelligent.

I realize that this can be carried too far, and nothing would be more annoying than to have a child sing while he is performing a piece he has already learned. But in practicing, singing aloud the melody that he is playing is often helpful.

Practicing in Phrases

Since music is made of groups of tones called phrases, each phrase expressing a musical idea, the student should study a phrase at a time, and not a succession of notes or measures. Neither should he play the piece over and over from beginning to end.

Often a child will start playing a piece and will stumble and make a mistake at the end of, say, the second line. Instead of stopping there and finding out what the trouble is and correcting that phrase, the tendency of many children is to begin the whole piece again, hoping by some lucky chance to get past the difficult spot which has never really been learned.

The teacher should impress on the child that spending his practice time in learning to play well half a dozen phrases of a piece is far better than superficially practicing the entire piece.

In practicing phrase by phrase, each new phrase, as it is learned, should immediately be played in context with the preceding ones. Sometimes, however, it is a good idea to practice phrases of similar construction that occur throughout the piece by removing them from their contexts and playing them in succession.

Learning a Piece Back End First

Here is a suggestion for practicing that I have used occasionally with children whose span of attention was short, and who could remember the beginning of a piece, but could not get to the end.

After the child has read the piece through to get the general idea of it, he begins by practicing the last phrase first. Suppose the piece was made of, say, six phrases. I mark them A B C D E F. The child learns phrase F first. Then he learns phrase E, and then puts E and F together. Then he learns Phrase D, and then plays D E F. He keeps up this procedure until he has learned phrase A.

The advantage of this method is that in playing the piece the child is always going toward familiar, rather than unfamiliar ground, which is comforting.

I tried this recently with Billy, a small boy who wanted to play "The Star-Spangled Banner" for his class to sing in school on Columbus Day. He was having difficulty playing the phrase that accompanies the words, "O say, does that star-spangled banner yet wave?" This is the longest and most difficult phrase in the piece. So, in order that he could bring the song to a confident conclusion, he practiced it back end first. We marked the whole piece in two-measure groups. Then he began practicing the last phrase, until he could play the music that goes with the words "and the home of the brave" with ease. Then he learned the music of "o'er the land of the free," and put the last two phrases together; then he tackled the music of "O say, does that star-spangled banner yet wave?" and when this was learned, he played to the end of the piece. Continuing this backward process, he learned "that our flag was still there." By practicing back end first, the difficult phrase was getting a great deal of attention, and very soon Billy was able to play our national anthem from beginning to end without losing his concentration, and was able to add his patriotic bit to the Columbus Day program.

Practicing back end first is useful, too, in learning a difficult passage. For example, the following passage has leaps that are rather wide for a small player to negotiate.

But it can easily be learned if practiced as follows:

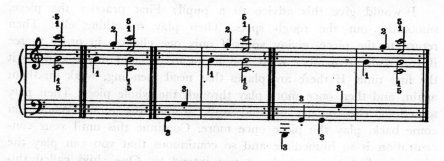

This method of practicing is also helpful for a more advanced student in dealing with long technical passages. The whole passage can be divided into convenient sections. The last section is learned first, then the last two, the last three, and so on, until the entire passage can be played fluently.

For example, the following run from the Mozart D minor Fantasy can be practiced as follows:

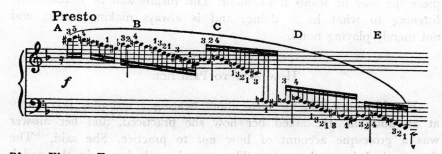

Play: First   **E**
Then   **D E**
Then   **C D E**
Then   **B C D E**
Finally **A B C D E**

Playing Correctly the First Time

Frequently a child will come to a lesson and play his piece for the teacher, making many mistakes, and will say with surprise and perfect candor, "I *do* know it! I played it yesterday without a mistake."

Now, this is literally true. But the question is, when did he play it perfectly? Probably after he had been practicing the piece ten to fifteen minutes. But what he has to learn is to play it perfectly the *first* time.

I would give this advice to a pupil: First practice the piece, smoothing out the rough spots. Then play something else. Then return to the piece, giving yourself only one chance, in order to see if you really remember what you mean to do, and if you can do it the first time. If there are places that need mending, work on them again, and then once more play through the whole piece. Then play something else, or get up and walk around the room. When you come back, play the piece once more. Continue this until your concentration is so immediate and so continuous that you can play the piece the first time exactly as you intend to. One child called this procedure the "Sandwich Method."

This way of practicing is absolutely necessary if a child or an adult is preparing to play in a recital. He must be confident that he can play his piece "without a mistake," that he can command everything, and can keep his mind entirely concentrated and his ears open.

To sum up, the student of any age should always practice his piece the way he wants it to *sound*. This means that he is constantly *listening* to what he is doing, and is always making music, and not merely playing notes.

How Not to Practice

Harold Bauer told me once about hearing a girl play very badly at an audition. He asked her how she practiced, and her answer was a grotesque account of how *not* to practice. She said, "The first week I learn the notes. The second week I put in the pedal. And the third week I put in the expression." (It sounded as though she were reading from a cookbook!) She had not the faintest conception that in practicing, notes, pedalling, and "expression" are inseparable. During her three weeks at the piano, music apparently had never been present.

A quality performance is not necessarily brought about by a great quantity of time spent in practicing, either. This was illustrated recently when I heard a young piano student play Weber's "Concertstück" in recital. Her performance, though facile, was so dull, it seemed to me as if it lasted for hours! After the concert I asked her how long she had been practicing this piece, and her answer was "All winter." Since the practicing of music, willy-nilly, involves making noises of one kind or another, I wondered how her family had endured living all winter while the playing of that long and singularly uninteresting composition was being perfected!

I sometimes ask my students to tell me not how *long* it took them to learn a piece, but how *short* it took them.

Do Not Practice Note by Note

Slow practicing is often desirable in order that you may hear every tone clearly. But it is undesirable if it results in destroying the continuity of the music.

I am reminded of how a celebrated pianist used to teach Bach's D major Prelude from the First Book of the "Well-Tempered Clavier." The student began by playing the Prelude through very slowly, holding each sixteenth note for the duration of a whole note. The fingers were to be raised high, and the tones were to sound exactly alike in volume. This trip through the Prelude took approximately an hour and a half!

After that, the student played the Prelude through once more, with the same mechanical touch, each sixteenth now being held for the value of a half-note. This, of course, took one-half the time— it took forty-five minutes. Then the piece was played in quarters, then in groups of two eighths, and finally in groups of four sixteenths. The emphasis had been entirely on the mechanics of performance. The student's fingers had no doubt been strengthened but unfortunately, during all this practice, he had never heard the Prelude as a piece of music. It was simply a gymnastic exercise.

The same displacement of emphasis was reported by a young theological student, studying the Book of Job in his seminary. He said that such minute and exhaustive attention was focused on each word that in the process "Job was lost." Because of the over-detailed practicing of the Prelude note by note as described above, "Bach was lost." Need I repeat that the student should practice phrase by phrase, rather than note by note?

Using the Metronome

The metronome is useful in establishing the over-all speed of a composition, if this has been indicated in the music by the composer or by an intelligent editor.

The metronome is also useful if you wish to find out whether you are playing faster today than you did last week. Checking with the metronome is an excellent way of discovering this entertaining fact.

The inventor of the metronome, Maelzel, presented one to his friend, Beethoven, who was delighted with it. Beethoven wrote a little canon, in which the voices imitate the steady tick-tock of the metronome, ending with the words, "Lieber, lieber Maelzel, leben sie wohl, sehr wohl!" Later, he used this tune as the motive of the Allegretto of the Eighth Symphony.

The speed of a composition is, of course, an integral part of the composer's intention, and Beethoven frequently wrote a metronome mark at the beginning of a movement to show its general speed. But he certainly could not have meant that the composition was to be played throughout in time with these inexorable nagging ticks.

Certain types of music could, conceivably, be played with a steady metronomic beat. But in general, music is so lovely and flexible a language, that it would be impossible for its rhythms to be forced into the rigidity of metronomic beats.

So, playing a piece straight through, endeavoring to keep in time with the metronome, is *not* recommended.

Practice Does Not Always Make Perfect!

Practicing is often a bugbear for many piano students because of the unfortunate connotation in their minds that practicing is the acquiring of skill merely by repeating the same thing over and over. A certain amount of repetition is, of course, necessary in order that a piece may be comprehended and memorized, and that technical habits may be formed. But making many repetitions is not necessarily practicing. I can furnish an autobiographical testimony to the musical futility of practicing by sheer repetition.

When I was a young student, I was learning the last movement of the Beethoven Sonata in C major, Op. 2, No. 3. There are fourteen short passages of sixth chords and octaves to be played staccato. These were difficult for me, and I bungled some of them at my lesson. My teacher told me that Henry, whose lesson preceded mine, was learning the same movement, and was also having difficulty with these passages. Being an excellent psychologist, she added that Henry was going to practice each of these places fifty times a day, and he was sure he could learn them in a week.

Not to be outdone by Henry, I decided immediately that I would practice each passage one hundred times a day! I did this for a week, playing each chord slowly, and with the exaggerated up and down wrist motion my teacher had taught me to use when playing staccato chords and octaves. The daily performance took four hours.

But, of course, it was impossible to concentrate on making these motions so many times. After two or three repetitions of a passage, my hands would move mechanically, without any mental effort on my part, and all I had to do was to keep on going and keep track of the number of repetitions. Since this process had no musical interest, I decided to use the time reading "David Copperfield," which *did* interest me.

So I propped the book up on the music rack, and began reading while I played. To keep the score straight, each time I finished a passage, I announced the number aloud, while continuing my reading. I would play a passage, saying aloud at the last note, "Fifty-eight," then repeat it, saying "Fifty-nine," and so on, for I could read several lines of the story while playing each passage through once. I went through this routine faithfully for a week.

On the last day, as I played the last note of the last passage, deliverance came! I had arrived at the point in the story where I exclaimed with Miss Trotwood, "Janet! Donkeys! One hundred!"

I was then well along in the story, and had read 188 pages of "David Copperfield." The passages were "ground" into my anatomy. But also "ground" into my system was the habit of playing without thinking, and without listening to the sounds that I was producing.

Such practicing put the emphasis solely on physical endurance. What a waste of time! What a disservice to Beethoven!

CONCLUSION

So we see that practicing includes such a variety of activities that we really need a "portmanteau word" that would cover the discipline of conquering the difficulties of piano playing, and the cultivation of an ever-enlarging understanding of the music that is being studied. In the final analysis we may say that practicing is learning how to interpret and how to play a musical composition.

MEMORIZING

MUSICAL MEMORY

When we play a piece from memory, we are traversing simultaneously several Paths of Remembrance:

Our *ears* are remembering the sound of the piece;

Our *fingers, hands, and arms* are remembering how we have habituated them to play the piece;

Our *eyes* may be remembering a picture of the printed page, though this is the least common Path of Remembrance;

Our *mind* is remembering what we have discovered of the content and structure of the music; and

We are also remembering the composition as an emotional experience.

"BECAUSE" — THE PROCESS OF ASSOCIATION

Perhaps you have mislaid a book. Some one in the family asks the slightly irritating question, "Where did you lose it?" or the more helpful one, "Where did you have it last?" You think back. You know you had it under your arm when you opened the front door, because you have a distinct recollection that it was in your way, as you turned the latch key. *Association* begins doing its perfect work! You go back to the front door, and find the book lying on the hall table.

All memorizing is a process of association. You recognize Mrs. Smith at a distance, because no one else could be associated in your mind with that funny-looking hat she has worn for years. In the same way, in music, you remember something *because* of something else.

A piece that has been taught intelligently by rote is, of course, already memorized, because the teacher has set up a series of associations in the student's mind and fingers that he is consciously following while he plays.

In memorizing a piece on his own, the student should try to discover and consciously set up for himself as many associations — as many "becauses" — as possible.

With little children memorizing a piece, these "becauses" may be very elementary. For instance, Stephen may remember that a piece begins on C A F, "because" he already knows the chord of F major, and there it is backwards! Or he may remember a measure "because" it begins with his third finger in each hand.

An older student may remember two passages that are similar, but not identical, because, although they start alike, at a certain point they diverge and move toward different endings. He will remember things that are different just because they *are* different.

CONCENTRATE ON CONTINUITY

A well-written composition is well-knit. Each musical idea is in some way either connected or contrasted with the others. The more a student can follow the pattern of the knitting (and not drop any stitches) the more secure his memorizing will be.

It is most important that there be no break in the continuity of the player's attention. This continuity is the life-line to which he clings, and there should be no weak places in it. If a piece is securely memorized, the player will be aware of what he *has* played, of what he *is* playing now, and of what he *will* play next. Thus he has a continuous realization of the context, and the piece unfolds itself consecutively. It is as though he were telling a story he remembers clearly from beginning to end.

MEMORIZING AS YOU GO ALONG

A teacher may assign a piece to a pupil, telling him to bring it back memorized — say, in a week. What many a student will do is to practice it from beginning to end, with the notes, from Monday to Thursday. Then, on Friday he will start memorizing, hoping to get the task completed in time for his piano lesson on Saturday afternoon. He has been a non-memorizer for four days, and a potential memorizer for one-and-a-half. It would have been far easier if he had started memorizing the piece on Monday.

Often a good plan in learning a new composition is first to play it all the way through to get the general sense, noticing parts that are alike and parts that are contrasted; then, to start at the beginning, practicing it phrase by phrase, and memorizing as you go along.

The first phrase should be studied carefully, until every detail is observed and heard, and the fingers can perform it accurately. Then the next phrase is memorized in the same way. The two phrases are compared, and then played from memory in succession. As the student studies each phrase, practices it, memorizes it, and adds it to the ones he knows, eventually the whole composition is memorized.

A piece is securely memorized when the player can think the piece through from beginning to end away from the piano, and when he is able to go to the instrument and begin playing at any point that he wishes.

When he first read the piece, it may have seemed to him a succession of unrelated parts. But after he has studied and memorized it, phrase by phrase, the piece becomes a whole, made of closely related ideas.

Part of Herbert Spencer's famous definition of Evolution includes these words: "Matter passes from an indefinite, incoherent homogeneity, to a definite, coherent heterogeneity."

The understanding of a piece of music follows something like the same evolution in the student's mind, as he goes from the first, undetailed, vague, over-all reading, to the final memorized performance, where details are present, but seen in relation to the whole. The music becomes in his mind coherent and shapely.

Most of us will have noticed a curious fact — that the better we know a composition, the shorter it seems to be. Ultimately, perhaps, we may come to think of it as an idea that exists without any time limitation whatsoever. For example, we can think of the Ninth Symphony or the Parthenon as Ideas — each a single unit not limited, in the one case, by Time, or in the other, by Space.

Don't Rely on Your Fingers Alone!

Many students think that if they repeat a passage, say ten times, it will certainly be memorized. It *may* be memorized technically, but sheer repetition of physical motions is the least reliable way of memorizing. If anything should happen to break the continuity of these motions, the student will be unable to continue. It would be disastrous if anyone joggled his elbow!

Unless the teacher is watchful, a child will often do his memorizing just this way. I, unfortunately, made frequent use of this method myself, as a little girl.

I remember so well trying to play a certain piece from memory, realizing that there was one passage that I had never really studied or understood, but believed I could play through, because I had played the notes correctly so many times. As I approached this spot, I would try to make my mind a blank, and literally prayed that I wouldn't think! I didn't want to interfere with all these motions that by now had become mechanical!

I really knew the music on either side of this danger spot, but as I neared it, I felt as though I were about to jump over a wide ditch. I was sure of the ground where I started my leap. But during the flight through uncharted space, I simply hoped for the best. If I reached terra firma on the other side, without having stopped playing, I gave a sigh of relief, and continued my journey to the end of the piece.

This, however, did not always work!

I remember one awful occasion when I was playing a Chopin waltz at an informal Pupils' Recital. There was one spot that I knew *I* didn't know, but I hoped that my *fingers* did! When I reached this place, I felt one of my fingers slipping; I grew panicky, and I did the last thing I intended to do — I began to *think!* I had struck a wrong chord. Startled by the strange sounds I was producing, my fingers balked completely. I came to a dead stop.

My teacher asked me to start the piece again. I doubted the wisdom of this suggestion, feeling sure that the cataclysm would occur again in the same place, but I began the piece once more. Again my fingers refused to carry me over the hurdle. I retreated in tears . . . I had nightmares in my sleep over this humiliating experience, and I have never liked that waltz since! It was many weeks before my confidence in playing from memory was restored.

In looking back, it seems to me that it was the teacher's business to have seen that I really knew the piece so well, before playing it in public, that even after a finger slip, I could have picked myself up and continued playing.

What to Do in Case of Trouble

In performance, the student should remember that, no matter what happens, he must keep his head and keep going. Once it has started, "the play must go on"! If he has played a "wrong note," he should disregard it, and continue playing just as though nothing unusual had happened. It is fatal for him to look back! Many people will forgive, and most people will not even notice a "wrong note," but everyone will notice if the pianist stops playing.

In practicing, it is useful to plan on certain "safety spots," to which you can jump in an emergency, leaving out in-between passages if necessary.

It is even better to be able to improvise a "filling," and play *something,* if your memory falters. This, of course, presupposes a familiarity with the language of music that should be a part of every piano student's equipment.

MEMORIZING FROM THE PRINTED PAGE, AWAY FROM THE PIANO

This way of memorizing demands the use of musical experience and imagination. As he works only from the printed page, the student must imagine the sounds represented by the notes, and imagine how he will play the piece technically.

Even children can learn to memorize in this way.

I remember a spectacular instance of this. One summer, after a busy teaching season, I went to Aeschi above Lake Thun to study with a remarkable musician, Johannes Schreyer of Dresden. One day he asked me if I would like to hear the lesson of another American, Leopold Mannes, a gifted little twelve-year-old boy. The next day I attended Leopold's lesson. As he entered the room, Schreyer said to Leopold, "Have you learned the Bach Three-Part Invention in D major?"

Leopold replied: "I only had two days, and there wasn't any piano I could use. But I learned half of it."

Schreyer continued: "I want you to *play* the two outer voices while you *sing* the middle voice. If you have studied it, of course you don't need the notes. Go to the piano, and transpose it into A major."

And Leopold did!

Later that summer, I visited Yorke Trotter at his London Academy of Music. He, too, believed that children should learn to memorize away from the piano.

I attended a class lesson of children ten or eleven years old. Dr. Trotter gave a bright little girl named Gladys a piece by Schytté, and told her to go into another room where there was no piano, and begin memorizing the piece.

In the meantime, the other children were "composing" at the piano. One child was asked to make up four measures of a sarabande. The next child added four of his own. Two other children followed, and, between them, they composed a sixteen-measure piece.

Then Gladys was sent for, and came bouncing into the room. She played the first page of the Schytté piece from memory without a slip!

It was all very impressive. Leopold and Gladys were, of course, musically gifted. But all children can develop, to a certain degree, this concentrated attention.

"A COUNTRY WALK"

I was teaching a group of children of "average" ability, and gave them a simple little piece, "A Country Walk," to memorize away from the piano. They were playing third-grade music, and this was a first-grade piece, which none of them had ever heard.

The group had done much ear training, so they had a fair idea of the sounds represented by the notes. They had analyzed many pieces, so they knew something of the construction of music.

A Country Walk

I gave the children copies of the piece, and asked them to study it, while sitting in their seats, and to stand up when they thought they could play it from memory.

Harriet, surprisingly, was the first to rise. She went to the piano and played the piece without faltering. She had learned the notes in exactly eight minutes!

She was an eager little girl with a good ear, but had not been an outstanding student in the group. So I was curious to know how she had memorized the piece correctly and so quickly. Harriet was a good "talker," and I asked her to tell the class how she had gone about learning the piece. She looked at the music and said:

"It was easy, because there was so much to remember it by." I asked her if she wouldn't tell us some of these "becauses" she had found so useful.

She started: "Well, some things you just have to plain remember. It's in C major — there's no 'because' about that. And the count is 'Four *One* Two Three' — there's no 'because' about that either!

"Of course, I looked the whole piece over first, to see what was easy. You play it almost all one hand at a time, and it's almost all made of eighths and quarters, and there's a lot of repetition and sequences."

The children were all looking at their own copies of the music while Harriet held forth. She continued:

"You remember the first line, because it sounds like the chord of C major all the way through, with some decorations. There's a passing note at the very beginning, where it goes E D C, and you finger it 3 2 1. The first two measures are the same, and then come two more measures, still around the chord of C.

"Then the second line is easy, because it starts with the same three notes that you did at the beginning, only this time you play it backwards, C D E with 1 2 3. You go in sequence right up the scale on every note from C to G. That's the first two measures. Then it sounds like the chord of G major, with some passing notes, and you're halfway through the piece."

Harriet continued her descriptive narrative down the page. When she came to the last line, she said, "I don't know the name of that fancy chord, but I can hear it in my head."

The class had been following Harriet's description with close attention. And when she had finished, three or four other children played the piece from memory. I did not take time to investigate *their* mental processes, but, at least, they had memorized it from the printed page!

Though the piece was very elementary, Harriet's account of how she had memorized it describes a process that an adult might use in memorizing much more difficult music.

CONCLUSION

Children, without realizing the sense of the words they use, often say, "I can play this piece by heart," meaning that they have memorized it. However, "playing by heart" is, in reality, the most important thing of all.

Everyone, from Harriet playing "A Country Walk" to Toscanini conducting a symphony, is having an emotional experience, and is really "playing by heart."

Every time you play a composition, you probably discover more of its emotional content, and this is added to your previous store of memories.

103

Memorizing

SOME ASPECTS OF
PIANO TECHNIQUE

AWARENESS

The acquiring of technique is the development of a communication system through which the music that you play enters the realm of sound.

The last outposts of this communication system between yourself and the music that you are producing on the piano are your hands and fingers. The lines of communication, extending from the fingertips to the shoulder-joints, must be free and open and responsive. Only when the system is in good working order is it possible for Music to come through.

The Chief Operators of this communication system are your ears, your mind, and your sensitivity to music. The ear is Operator No. 1, and it should always be alert and active. Your mind, Operator No. 2, should be following with continuing attention and interest the unfolding of the music that you are playing. Operator No. 3, your sensitivity to music, is your emotional enjoyment, as the "imprisoned splendor" of the music is being released while you play.

If, while you are playing, the attention of these operators should wander from the music to something quite outside the situation, your arms and hands, from sheer force of habit, will probably go on playing, and your fingers will act like well-trained automatons. But, during this hiatus, *you* will have had no part in the making of the music. You will neither hear what you are doing, nor know what you are doing, nor enjoy what you are doing. And your communication lines will have been reduced to something as far removed from your awareness as the music rack or the legs of the piano. You will, of course, be making sounds, but to a sensitive listener, you will not be making Music.

When your communication system is working, however, besides your awareness through hearing, knowing, and enjoying the music that you are playing, there can also be another awareness — the conscious pleasure in the feeling in your fingers, hands, and arms, when they are entirely coordinated with the three Operators in producing music. When you are aware of the feeling in your body, there will be a sense of ease, of physical efficiency, a joy of physical well-being in your piano playing.

Any athlete whose body is perfectly coordinated experiences this delightful sensation of physical efficiency. Babe Ruth, for instance, certainly must have felt conscious *physical* pleasure when, on hearing the convincing "ping" as his bat sent the ball soaring into space, he realized that he had hit another home run, and began his victorious journey around the bases. He was aware that his baseball-playing technique was in perfect order and entirely adequate. And his three Operators were all aware of what was going on. His ear was delighted to hear the sound of the bat on the ball. His mind realized that the Yankees were one step nearer to winning the game. And his sensitivity to the beauties of the game of baseball was probably stimulated.

In the case of the piano student, the acquiring of physical awareness and coordination is the reason for developing piano technique. This brings technique into its proper place in the full circle of performance. Studying technique is not following a prescribed method of playing the piano. It is developing a physical awareness and coordination that will make possible the release of Music.

POSTURE

In order to insure a sense of physical freedom, the pianist must be aware first of his posture at the piano.

Any golfer knows that it is necessary to get a good stance, and to have his whole body well balanced before he swings the club. The pianist, too, must realize that his body must be well balanced before he begins to play.

An object is balanced if it is so centered that movement in every direction is possible. The pianist will have to experiment to discover, to a nicety, exactly where he will sit in relation to the keyboard. This means that he must consider two things: the height of the chair, and its distance from the piano.

If his seat is too *low,* or if he succumbs to the temptation of sitting in a comfortable slump, leaning against the back of the chair, his arms and hands will be pulled away from the keyboard.

If he is sitting too *close,* his elbows will stick out akimbo, and his upper arms will be of no use to him. It will be impossible for him to make a round *fortissimo* tone without banging. He will have to exert *force* instead of using the *power* that could come through if his body were well poised and his arms were free.

If, however, the chair is at the right height, and he pushes it back and sits erect on the front of it, at a comfortable distance from the keys, his body will be well balanced, and he will be able, if he wishes, to throw his weight forward onto his fingertips, and also to move his arms freely over the keyboard.

GET ACQUAINTED WITH YOUR ARMS!

Many piano students seem to feel that when they practice they must be strict disciplinarians of their obstinate hands and fingers and must force these reluctant members to play. As a result of this, their whole "machine" is tense and rigid, and the tones that they produce on the piano are hard and strident.

Finger control and agility must, of course, be cultivated. But I have found that many students who have great facility, but little tonal variety, concentrate almost exclusively on facile finger action, leaving untapped the many resources of their arms.

A good way to begin investigating these resources and to become conscious of the possibilities of the arms in piano playing is to compare the motion of the elbow-joint with that of the shoulder-joint.

Try doing it this way: Extend your right arm in front of you, palm upward, and hold a pencil horizontally in a loose fist. Bend the arm at the elbow, so that the fist is pointing upward toward the ceiling. Put your left hand underneath the elbow, so that it supports the weight of the arm. Keep the forearm in this vertical position. Then, slowly and without straining, using the elbow-joint as a pivot, rotate the forearm as far as possible to the left and to the right. Although there will be a certain "give" at the wrist-joint, the motion is all generated at the elbow. You can gauge the amount of rotary motion of which the elbow-joint is capable by watching the pencil as your forearm turns in each direction. Notice how far the pencil moves as the elbow rotates.

Next, stretch the unsupported right arm out full length in front of you, still holding the pencil lightly. Again, rotate the arm slowly, left and right, but this time move, not from the elbow, but only from the shoulder-joint. Watch the pencil and notice how much farther it travels in each direction when the movement originates at the shoulder instead of at the elbow. The reason, of course, is a physiological one: the ball-and-socket shoulder-joint permits free movement in every direction. The elbow-joint works primarily as a hinge, but a degree of rotation of the forearm is possible.

In getting acquainted with his "machine" the pianist should begin by exploring these possibilities of arm movement.

LET YOUR UPPER ARM DO IT! POWER VERSUS FORCE

Do not send a boy to do a man's work! Do not make ineffective movements with your fingers, stretching them unmercifully in the effort to reach distant keys, when your upper arm, working from your shoulder-joint, can carry your hand quickly and easily from one place on the keyboard to another. Do not try to make wide leaps on the keyboard by moving the forearm from the elbow. Wide leaps can be made much more swiftly and accurately by moving the upper arm from the shoulder-joint. For instance, compare the speeds of these two motions:

First, put your right hand third finger on middle C and, moving the forearm from the elbow-joint, play the C three octaves above.

Second, play the same two C's, but this time move the whole arm from the shoulder-joint. Notice how much more quickly and securely the measurement from key to key is made when you use the *whole* arm.

When Boulder Dam was being built, I remember watching with admiration the performance of a huge portable crane. It was supposed to pick up an enormous load of iron from the floor and place it somewhere else, and this is what happened:

The engineer, sitting in his cabin, controlled the movements of the crane by a system of levers and wires and pulleys. After starting up his engine, he pulled a particular lever, and the arm of the crane swung around until it was directly over the weight to be lifted. A huge hook at the end of a steel rope descended from the crane in a perfectly straight line, and attached itself to the load of iron. The engineer pulled another lever, and the arm of the crane lifted the load from the floor as though it were a feather, and swung off with it until the load was exactly over its new destination. Then, because the engineer knew his job, and the alignment was perfect, the arm descended and the load was placed in the exact spot where it was supposed to land.

I thought at the time that the crane was probably delighted to do so much with so little effort, and was very glad that the engineer knew so well how to direct its motions!

You are the engineer of your piano-playing "machine." In order to play efficiently, there must be a constant adjustment at the shoulder-joint. As the arm of the crane travels from place to place, so your arm must travel, constantly shifting and adjusting, in order to keep the hand directly opposite whatever keys are to be played.

HANDS

Hands are wonderful! How much is communicated by a handshake, ranging from an iron grip like that of the statue of the Commendatore in "Don Giovanni" to the languid limpness of a Lydia Languish!

A masseuse once told me, when I commented on her sensitive and capable hands, that they generated a great deal of electricity, and because of this, she could communicate to me much of her own vitality. She said that at the training school she had attended, tests were given to the applicants to discover the amount of electricity they had in their hands. I cannot imagine a more gracious gift than the "laying on of hands."

In piano playing there is the most intimate contact between your hands and fingers and the keyboard. Hands should not be stretched mercilessly, nor allowed to be either devitalized or tense and rigid. Never play when your hands are cold. If you do so, you are very apt to strain them, as you cannot sensitively feel what they are doing.

A good way to make your hands feel warm and alive is to place the palm of the right hand crossways on the palm of the left. Then move the palms briskly and lightly, with a circular motion, as though you were molding a lump of putty into a soft ball. This will make your hands feel warm and vital.

Many pianists, before playing a recital, plunge their hands into hot water above the wrist. This stimulates circulation in hands and arms, and reduces possible nervous tension.

Hands should be treated with respect and consideration and affection.

Securing Good Hand Position

The object of the following exercise is to center weight on the five fingertips.

Sitting comfortably, rest the right forearm on a table, with the hand forming a lightly-closed fist, and with the thumbside upward. Then rotate the arm inward toward the thumbside of the fist. The length of the forearm, the under-part of the wrist, the second joints of the fingers, and the side of the thumb are all now touching the table. The thumb is slightly curved. Now, with the forearm, wrist, and thumb still touching the table, very slowly uncurl the other fingers. At first your fingernails will scrape against the table, but continue the uncurling movement until you can feel the sensitive pads of the fingertips as the knuckles rise and the hand forms an arch. Keep the fingers curved, so that the joints at the tips do not bend in. Tilt the hand slightly toward the thumb. Now, very slowly, tilt the weight forward onto the fingertips by raising the whole arm from the shoulder-joint until the wrist is about two inches above the table. The thrust of the shoulder and the weight of the arm are now centered on the tips of all five fingers, and you have a good hand position for playing. Your arm and hand are now something like a flying buttress. In Gothic architecture, the weight of the roof is supported by the walls, but is also carried to the ground by means of the flying buttresses. Everything is in a state of complete and effortless equilibrium.

Weight-Touch and Strengthening the Fingertips

Now that you have secured a good hand position, you can strengthen each finger by allowing the weight of the hand and arm to center on each fingertip in turn. Begin by putting the weight on all five fingertips as described above. Take the weight from the thumb, lifting it only far enough to clear the table. Keep the thumb in this position. The weight is now distributed between the other four fingertips. Then slowly raise in turn the fifth, fourth, and second fingers from their contact with the table. Since only the third finger is now touching the table, the entire weight of hand and arm is now centered on this fingertip. (The third finger is the easiest to begin with, in learning to center the weight on each finger in turn, because it is the central point of balance in the hand and arm. One child remarked while doing this exercise, "I feel like a table with one leg in the middle!")

Keeping the weight on the third finger, slowly let the thumb touch the table again, letting the weight distribute itself between two points — the first and third fingertips. Then add the fifth finger. You now have the shape of a triad under your hand.

Experiment in putting the weight on every combination of fingertips in turn, until finally the fourth and fifth fingers individually will accept the responsibility of bearing the weight of the hand and arm without collapsing at the tip-joint.

Do not push into the table. Just let the weight balance comfortably on the sensitive cushions at the fingertips. (Fingernails are not sensitive, and we are trying to develop sensitivity as well as strength, so the nails must be short, otherwise the fingers will "skate" around, and the tip-joint will certainly collapse.)

Later, if you practice finger exercises with action from the knuckles, and the finger still bends at the tip, go through the above routine again, concentrating on the weak finger.

Arm Weight versus Featherweight

Once the feeling of arm weight on the fingertips is realized, you must cultivate the exact opposite, which is lightness of the arm and hand.

Again, balance the weight of the arm on the third finger. Then, without disturbing the alignment of hand and arm, and still touching the table, withdraw the weight of the upper arm and forearm and lightly lift the other fingers as high as possible. Your hand and arm will be poised delicately on the tip of the third finger, and will feel as light as thistledown. Now lift the arm from the shoulder-joint until the third finger has cleared the table. Do not hunch up the shoulder, and do not let the hand hang limply from the wrist. Arm and hand are in one piece. Now move the arm several times up and down through the air, feeling that the motion is effortless.

After balancing the third finger on the table with a light arm, stand up, and balance in turn each fingertip of one hand on the flat palm of the other hand. Alternate between the touch where the weight of the arm centers on the fingertip, and the light arm touch. The feeling in your palm is entirely different: in the first case, you will feel pressure; in the second, you will hardly be aware of the touch of the finger. This exercise helps you to discover just how much weight you are using, and to change quickly from a heavy to a light arm. In playing, this change of touch sometimes has to be made within a single phrase, if the tone qualities of the music demand it.

Weight touch will produce a warm, round tone in melody playing. It is also the best way of playing chords, when you wish a full, non-percussive sound.

A light arm is essential in much *pianissimo* playing, and also where the fingers must scamper as fast as possible. If you are going to race over the keys, of course you will "lay aside every weight," especially the weight of your upper arm!

The pianist should have at his command many ways of touching the keys. Each of these will produce a different tone quality. The essential thing is that he knows what mechanism to use in order to produce the particular tone quality that he wishes. Piano music is infinitely varied. It demands many varieties of tone, which can be produced only by the many varieties of touch that should be part of every pianist's technical equipment.

FROM SHOULDER TO FINGERTIPS

Quite different tone qualities are produced by what is called a "slow hammer" or a "quick hammer." If the finger action on the key is sharp and quick, the hammer will strike the string with a sharp, quick blow, and the tone will be brilliant. If, on the contrary, the key is depressed slowly, the hammer will move slowly and give the string a gentle push, instead of a quick stroke, and you will produce a warm, singing tone.

To produce this singing tone, experiment as follows: touch a white key silently with the second finger held rather flat; the arm is held level. Now depress the key slowly by moving the arm slightly up and forward. The weight of the arm will first be on the flat of the finger, then as the arm movement continues, the weight is rolled forward onto the cushion and finally onto the tip of the finger. Do not continue the arm movement beyond the point where the weight is balanced on the tip, or you will over-balance. Even though you feel that most of the activity is in the fingertip, the motion originates at the shoulder-joint.

It is as difficult to describe a sensation as to describe a perfume, but perhaps this sensation of rising on the fingertip can be compared to the feeling in your feet when, from a standing position, you slowly rise on tiptoe. It takes many words to describe an uncomplicated motion that can be demonstrated at the keyboard or on a table in a moment.

This deliberate motion of the arm rising and rolling the weight forward onto the fingertips, can produce a round and singing tone in playing a curving melody. Here the whole group of tones will be made with one continuous rising motion, as the weight is transferred from one fingertip to the next. In order to explore this, place the right hand first, second, and fifth fingers silently on E, G, and C, then press the keys in turn with a continuous rising motion of the arm. E will be played on the side of the thumb, G on the cushion of the second finger, and C on the tip of the fifth. By making a continuous arm movement, you can produce a legato crescendo. (The forward and upward arm motion must not be confused with the suggestion for playing rolled chords with a rotary arm motion, described later in this chapter. That tone is quite different.)

This touch is also useful for training the left hand fifth finger to give full value to a low bass note, thus making a sustained sound in playing a broken chord accompaniment, or a jumping bass. If you can take time to feel that your fifth fingertip has the sensation of "suction" on the key, you will be producing a sustained tone. In playing a jumping bass, as in a Chopin waltz, we all know how a young student will tend to scant the length of the tone on the first bass note of the measure in his eagerness to get up to the following chord. But these bass tones are very important. If played in succession, they form a melody in their own right. Each one "sets" the harmony of its own measure.

It is a good idea to play these bass notes in succession in the speed of the waltz, leaving out the chords. Each tone will be held for three counts. Technically, play each note with the touch described above, letting the arm and hand rise slightly up and forward onto the cushion of the fifth fingertip. Later, when you play the complete left-hand part, you will make less motion, but before playing the chords, do allow the fifth fingertip to cling to each key until you have heard the tone and can connect it in your mind with the following low bass note. The motion must not, of course, be exaggerated or the rhythm of the bass will be distorted.

Distributing the Weight Between Different Parts of the Hand

It is frequently the case that one hand has to play both melody tones and accompanying tones. The melody tones should, of course, be more prominent, and the accompanying tones softer. This can most easily be done by distributing the weight within the hand, centering it on the fingers that play the melody, and lightening it from the other fingers.

A slight rotation of the arm at the shoulder-joint, tilting the hand either inward or outward, will put the weight of the arm on the melody tones where you wish it and will keep it away from the fingers where weight would make too loud a tone.

An excellent example where both hands are employed in this way is "From Strange Lands and People," the first piece in Schumann's "Scenes from Childhood." If the hands are slightly tilted toward the little finger sides, the arm weight can produce excellent melody lines, and no weight will be on the thumbs. These unruly members then will not interfere with the movement of the melodies, but will do what they are expected to do, which is to complete the harmony and to supply rhythmic interest to this charming little piece.

Other familiar examples occur in Schumann's little pieces for young students from the "Album for the Young": "The Little Romance" and "The Happy Farmer" (middle part). Also, the "Entreating Child" and "Happiness" from the "Scenes from Childhood," and the "Cradle Song" Op. 124, No. 6. These pieces can be played much more easily if the weight is distributed as suggested, than if the hand were held level and some fingers were obliged to play louder than others.

In hymns the two most important voices are usually the soprano and the bass. If arm weight is directed slightly toward the little finger sides of both hands, these voices can be brought out with a good tone and with little effort.

In any contrapuntal passage where two voices are played by one hand, and one is to be more prominent than the other, it is most helpful to make an analysis of how the weight can best be distributed to bring out the more important line.

The same principle holds good in playing chords, where one voice is to be more prominent than the others.

It is interesting to experiment with a single chord of three or four notes played by either hand, centering the weight on each finger in turn in order to bring out a different voice. For instance, play this chord three times: right hand, Eb-Ab-C, with the first, third, and fifth fingers. Rotating the upper arm at the shoulder, direct the arm weight first toward the thumb; then repeat the chord letting the weight center in turn on the third and fifth fingers. Listen to the dynamic balance as each tone in turn comes to the forefront of the harmonic mass.

Experiment with the left hand in the same way, playing, for example, the chord E-G♯-B-D with fingers 5 3 2 1, letting the weight of the arm center on each finger in turn. In studying the distribution of weight in the hand, be careful not to play chords that involve the slightest feeling of strain or stretching of the hand. Any group of keys that your hand can cover comfortably will make an interesting proving ground for this kind of experiment in distribution of weight and tonal balance.

THE POSITION OF THE WRIST

With either a heavy or a light arm, the best position for the wrist is slightly higher than the hand. In using weight touch, a slightly raised wrist will make it possible for weight to travel easily from the shoulder to the fingertips, and you can produce a full, round tone. If the wrist is held *lower* than the knuckles, the hand is at a disadvantage, because the stream of energy coming down your arm will settle at the lowest point, which will be the wrist-joint, just as water always seeks its lowest level. When the wrist is at its lowest, you have very little control of your fingers on the keyboard.

A convincing way to help a pupil whose wrist is too low to realize just where his weight is being centered is to pull his hand away from the piano when he is playing. You can do this with practically no effort. His hand will slide onto his lap, and he will probably be very surprised to see how little control he has over his fingers when his wrist is in this low position. If his wrist is still low and you pull his hand away from the keyboard a second time, he will probably resist by stiffening the arm and hand and clutching the keys with his fingers vigorously, as though he were hanging on to a trapeze. But if his wrist is slightly *higher* than the hand, the weight of his hand and arm will be balanced forward on his fingertips, and you cannot easily pull his hand off the keys.

Very occasionally a low wrist is helpful in playing certain measures. An instance occurs in the Beethoven Sonata in A major, Opus 2, third movement, Trio, measures 18 to 22. Here the left hand fifth finger has to hold the E below middle C, while an octave above it, the other fingers of the hand play D E, C E, B E, A E, legato. If the wrist is held very low and is swung inward toward the thumb, the tip of the fifth finger can cling to the upper corner of the low E, while the other fingers are playing. Even a small hand can play the passage if the wrist is held in this position, whereas it would be impossible for the fingers to reach the keys if the wrist were held high. The distance between the low E and the higher D is easily negotiable if the wrist is held low rather than high. In general, however, the most advantageous position for the wrist is slightly higher than the hand.

Try to avoid unnecessary motion of the wrists. For example, it is wasteful to allow the wrist to collapse and rise again while playing a single tone or chord. It may make *you* feel different, but it has no possible effect on the tone that you have produced. The hammer has struck once for all, and nothing that you can do to the *key* can change the vibrations of the strings that you have set in motion. The factors that do affect tone are the speed with which the hammer sets the string in motion (this is determined by the speed with which the key is depressed by your finger), the amount of force with which it is depressed, overtones from the other strings, half-pedal, etc. The only point that is being discussed here is that a wobbly wrist motion on a single key may give a physical and psychical experience of pleasure to the player, but cannot possibly affect the quality of sound, or change the vibrations of the strings, once the hammer has set them in motion.

Another unwise wrist motion that is sometimes advocated is that of lifting the arm at the end of every phrase, with the hand hanging limply. Musically, this motion often produces a distortion of meaning, since the gesture is a negative one and frequently the last tone of a phrase is its most positive. Also, this gesture breaks up the continuity of the music. Technically, it is an inefficient way of playing, because the hand is alternately collapsing and then recovering to begin the next phrase.

Both of these exaggerated wrist motions are usually made to acquire what the student believes to be relaxation. But, to my mind, they produce only devitalization.

The wrist sometimes has a major role to play in piano playing, particularly in octave passages and chord passages. But, in general, I think that its role is one of being supple and responsive, but quiet. It should not take the center of the stage by being exaggeratedly high or low, or by moving around too much. In piano playing, your wrist should feel neither strained nor inert, but alive and competent, and always within the sphere of your awareness.

WHERE TO PLAY ON THE KEY

When a little boy first plays the piano, he is apt to think that when he pushes a key down the sound he makes comes from something directly beneath his fingertips. If the piano is a grand, it is a good idea to show him, at his first lesson, how it "works." He must learn that the sound is produced far back, inside the piano, by a vibrating string (or set of unison strings). The white keys he touches are usually 18 inches long, and the black keys are two inches shorter. Attached to the far end of each key are a damper and a hammer. As he presses the key down, two things happen: The damper which has been touching the string rises so as to allow the string room to vibrate. The hammer moves up and strikes the string, which begins at once to vibrate, and then the hammer drops back into its place. When he releases the key, the damper falls on the vibrating string and the tone ceases.

The piano key is really a lever. When you press a key down at the front end, the leverage is greatest. Since the key resistance is lightest, a slight pressure will cause the damper to rise and the hammer to strike the string. As you move toward the fall-board (where Mr. Steinway and other piano makers sign their names), the resistance becomes progressively heavier, and you have to use more weight or exert more pressure to produce the tone. Perhaps you remember playing see-saw as a child. When you sat at the very end of the board, the leverage was very great, and the weight of your body would send the person who was sitting on the other end up in the air. But the nearer you sat toward the middle of the board, the more difficult it was to get the see-saw moving.

The action of a piano key is similar to that of a see-saw. The piano student should experiment, moving a single finger from the front to the back of both white and black keys. Notice how much more pressure is required to depress the keys at the back ends.

Since the shape of the hand is as it is (the first and fifth fingers being shorter than the others), and since the black keys are back where they are (and are shorter than the white keys), the pianist must be aware of just where his finger is touching each key.

When the thumb and fifth fingers play white keys all five fingers can play on the forward ends of the keys, where the resistance is lightest. However, when both thumb and fifth finger play black keys, the other three fingers will play further back toward the fall-board.

For instance, in playing the F♯ minor triad (F♯-A-C♯) with the right hand first, third, and fifth fingers, the third finger must play far back on A, because of the position of 1 and 5 on the short black keys. Notice how much heavier the action is under the third finger than under the first and fifth.

When either thumb or fifth finger is on a black key and the other fingers are playing white keys, the hand must be adjusted to bring the fingers into the most comfortable position. You will find that the hand can shuttle very quickly forward and back if the arm is kept in a straight line from fingertips to shoulder. This insures that the line of the knuckles will always be parallel with the line of the front edges of the keys, and that there will be no waste motion caused by awkward turning at the wrist or elbow.

The following exercise, if transposed into all keys, using the same fingering as in the key of C, will give the student experience in making these in-and-out adjustments. This involves many combinations of the fingers on black and white keys.

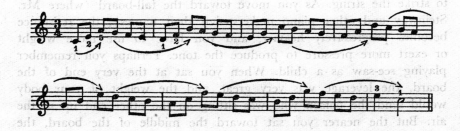

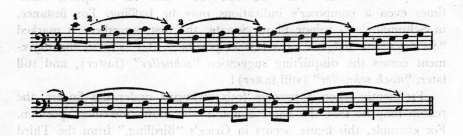

Play the exercise as a slow, expressive melody, transferring weight from one fingertip to the next. After playing first the right hand, then the left hand, in the key of C (as given above), continue playing this exercise in D-flat, D, and so on, chromatically through all the keys, using the same fingering. Listen carefully to the tone quality you are producing and be aware of the differences in key resistance as your hand shifts on the keyboard. Let the arm travel freely from the shoulder-joint, following the direction of the melodic movement. The hand should always be directly opposite the keys that are to be played, so there should be no awkward sideways motion of the wrist. The weight of the hand and arm should be centered accurately on each fingertip in turn, and the line of the knuckles should be kept parallel to the front edges of the keys.

After playing the exercise as a slow, expressive melody, change the touch completely. With the lightest arm, play the exercise as fast as possible, *pianissimo,* in C major through two octaves. Play on the tips of the keys where the key resistance is uniformly light.

Experiment with two contrasting *pianissimo* touches. First play with "close fingers," keeping the fingertips close to the keys throughout. Then play with "high fingers," raising each one, and articulating well from the knuckle-joints. Listen most carefully to the contrasting tone qualities that these two touches produce. With the "close finger" touch, the tones purr along very legato, as though you were stroking velvet. With the "high finger" touch, the tones glint like drops of water falling in sunlight. Be sure to hear the tiny percussive click as each fingertip strikes a key.

It takes about 12 minutes to complete this routine. It will prove to be excellent for "warming up" ears, hands, and fingers at the beginning of the practice period.

In practicing this exercise with a light arm, play as fast as possible, but not faster than possible—in other words, play no faster

than you can hear each tone that you make. As to speed, sometimes even a composer's indications may be baffling. For instance,
in Schumann's G minor Piano Sonata, the first movement is marked
"So rasch wie möglich" (as fast as possible). But later in the movement comes the disquieting suggestion *"schneller"* (faster), and still
later, *"noch schneller"* (still faster)!

Frequently when a passage feels awkward under the fingers, the
reason may be that the hand is not in the most convenient position.
For example, this figure occurs in Grieg's "Birdling," from the Third
Book of Lyric Pieces:

The fingers of the left hand can, of course, play on the front of
the keys. And in the right hand it would be easy to play A F D
on the front of the keys, if it were not for the B♭. But, when that
is added, A and F must be played much farther back. Prepare
the hand-shape necessary for the entire right-hand group, by touching all four keys before starting to play the figure.

Passages like the following, from the Russian folk-tune "Song
of the Boatman," can easily be played legato if the hand is set far
back and kept there.

Begin by placing 2, 4, and 5 on F♯, A, and B, back toward the fall-
board, and the thumb on D but close to the edge of the D♯. This will
make it possible for the thumb to play the black key (D♯) without turning the wrist. As one child described it, "You can't play this piece in the
open road — you have to go back, in among the daisies!"

Playing the interval from B to G legato will be made easy if the
arm rotates inward, carrying weight from the fifth finger on B, across the
two black keys, to the fourth finger on G.

Other awkward passages in more difficult music can often be played with ease if you analyze where the fingers will play most comfortably along the length of the keys, and then prepare a group of notes at a time.

CHOICE OF FINGERING

Since your actual contact with the piano keys is made through your fingertips, the choice of the fingering you use is highly important.

Piano music, whether played by a child or a concert artist, can not sound musically intelligent or be played with freedom unless the fingering and hand shifts coincide with the phrasing and the musical contours. The choice of the fingers that you use may be conditioned by the size and shape and length of fingers of your own hand. Fingering is an intimate thing; there is no inflexible rule of fingering for all hands, and all hands may not be able to finger a passage the same way.

But the phrase is always master of the musical situation, and you must adapt your fingering to the phrasing of the passage, as you understand it. The best way to do this is to cover as many keys of the phrase as make a comfortable handful, and then shift to the next position needed. The best fingering will be that which produces the phrases and musical contours with the greatest economy of adjustment and the minimum of hand shifting.

A few instances of bad fingering are running short of fingers, playing large intervals with fingers that have only a short reach, and choosing fingering necessitating awkward turns of the hand in the middle of the phrase.

After you have explored a passage and have decided what is best for your hand, stick to the fingering that you have chosen. If, later, you decide on some other fingering, stick to that until you find something better still. And always be prepared to change your mind.

This point of view is advocated by Busoni. He writes in the Preface of his edition of the Bach Inventions: "*At present,*" (my italics) "I change fingers on repeated notes, little or not at all."

It is interesting to compare the fingering of compositions as edited by different pianists. For example, compare the fingering of Beethoven sonatas as edited by Liszt, d'Albert, Heinrich Germer, von Bülow, Tovey, and Schnabel—or the works of Chopin as edited by Joseffy, Cortot, or Paderewski.

There is much to be learned from each of these editions. Each editor is endeavoring to clarify the situation according to his own musical interest and understanding. All these editions are the work of pianists who were also reverent students of the music they sought to interpret. It is fascinating to make comparisons between them; and then, as regards the detail of fingering, to try to discover the musical reasons that led each to his choice of fingering.

GESTURE

"Straight is the line of duty, but curved is the line of beauty."

Beautiful melodies express themselves largely in curves, and the most beautiful often in double curves. To *see* the curves in a printed melody, draw a continuous line connecting the heads of the notes in each phrase. This gives you a visual sense of the shape of the tune and the balance of the curves.

A delightful example of melodic curves is the Londonderry Air, which is considered one of the most beautiful of melodies. Here is the melodic contour of the first phrase:

Here is the curve in relation to its median line, which represents the key-note:

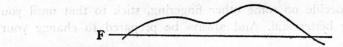

And this is the melodic contour of the last two phrases of the melody:

Notice the dramatic intensity of the curve as the tune swings from C to its highest point A. Then the tune curves downward, resting for a moment on the key-note F. In the final phrase, the melody makes a double curve up to D, then down to the octave D below, and at last, with an upward turn, comes to rest on the key-note F.

Contour is inherent within a melody. In playing this or any other melody, the hand and arm should adapt themselves to the melodic curves. This bodily adaptation I call "Gesture."

A melody is not a succession of detached tones. You do not play this note *and* this note *and* the next; but this note *to* this note *to* the following one. Your arms and hands yield to the melodic movement and follow its lead, much as you would follow your partner's lead in a dance.

All gesture derives from the music itself, and is not something you apply to the music.

Playing Rolled Chords

Arm rotation from the shoulder is particularly useful in playing wide rolling chords where the notes are out of the reach of the fingers. The Schumann "Nachtstück" in F major, Op. 23, No. 4, has in the right hand a succession of rolled chords. The first phrase of the melody is given below:

Try playing the first chord with a slow, continuous rotary motion of the arm, and notice what happens. After playing the thumb on F, the weight of the second finger on C is at first directly on the center of the tip, then it gradually shifts until you feel that it is transferred to the outer edge of the fingertip, as the arm rotates to bring the fifth finger over A. As the A is pressed down, let the gesture "follow through," until the hand is balanced on the outer edge of this finger. The hand should be relaxed, but not collapsed.

As the arm travels, each finger in turn catches the weight, as would the spokes of a slowly revolving wheel.

In analyzing the gesture of rolling this chord, it may be helpful to place your left hand on your right forearm, to feel the "track" of the movement, as your arm rotates slowly from left to right. This will perhaps give you the same sort of sensation that you feel when you see a slow-motion picture of a person diving or a horse jumping. Your left hand is in the role of the spectator. When the chord is played in time, the movement of course quickens.

While you are investigating any gesture, be sure to hear the tone qualities that you are producing; in the Schumann piece, listen to the changing harmonies under the melody tone A. Notice how well you can control the tone quality by carefully graduating the amount of weight that you center on each finger.

Notice also how the "color" of the tone A changes in the three rolled chords. Even the pitch seems to change as we hear A in a different relationship to the root of each harmonic mass. In the first chord, A is the third of the F major triad, and sounds rather high. In the second chord, A is the root of the dominant seventh and sounds relatively lower. Finally, in the third chord, A is the fifth of the D minor triad, and sounds highest of all.

Rotary gesture in rolled chords cannot possibly hurt the hand, whereas stretching the fingers from key to key is apt to strain both hand and arm. Many a hand has been permanently injured by doing old-fashioned stretching exercises, where the hand was, for example, held rigid on a five-note diminished-seventh chord, and each finger in turn was forced to play each key *fortissimo* many times, while the other fingers were holding the other keys down firmly. This kind of exercise may strengthen individual fingers, but the strain on the hand is tremendous. For most hands, stretching exercises should be done sparingly, if at all, and the resources of rotary motion should be investigated.

Pivotal Motion

The "Aeolian Harp" Etude of Chopin, Op. 25, No. 1, can be played without fatigue, even by small hands, if the inherent movement of the music itself is allowed to dictate the natural gesture to be used in playing.

Throughout the piece an accompaniment of broken chords in contrary motion is given to the two hands. This contrary motion can be expressed by the gesture of the arms. The elbows can move freely toward and away from the body, while each wrist acts as a sort of pivot. As the arms yield themselves to the contours of the music, each finger in turn is brought directly over the key that it is to play, and no stretching is necessary.

The basic gesture in playing this piece is the pivotal movement of the arms. Once this is established, you can use a light arm for delicacy of tone, or finger-stroke for greater brilliance in the melody line.

The Schumann Romanza in F-sharp major, Op. 28, No. 2, can also be played with ease if a pivotal arm motion is used. In the first section, the technical problem is that the melodies in the right and left hands must sound very legato, even though they must be played almost entirely with the thumbs. If the thumbs *strike* the keys, the melody tones will be detached, instead of legato. If, however, the thumbs are kept close to the keys, the arms with a pivotal motion can draw the thumbs sideways from one key to the next, following the shape of the melody. A skillful use of the pedal is an additional help in securing a good legato.

Matching Repeated Figures

Gesture of another kind will help in outlining the contour of the melodic figures in the Scherzo of the Beethoven Sonata in A major, Op. 2, No. 2.

Each figure is an ascending broken chord, ending with a whipped-off staccato note. Musically, the figures in the two hands "match," much as in the orchestra the violins may be imitated by the 'cellos. Pianistically, the figures in the right hand fit the hand and arm. The gesture of the right arm *away* from the body, *toward* the fifth finger, is easy and natural. When the same figure occurs in the left hand, it must be played with equal facility, even though the movement of the arm *toward* the body and *toward* the thumb is not easy and not natural.

If a similar gesture is used in each hand, the figures will match, and the imitation will be well brought out. In playing the right-hand figure, try tipping the hand *away* from the thumb, playing on the outer edges of the fingers, while the arm rotates *away* from the body. In playing the left-hand figures, tip the hand *toward* the thumb, and play on the inner edges of the fingers, while the arm rotates *toward* the body.

Impressionistic Music

Quite different will be the gestures in playing a piece like Debussy's "Girl With the Flaxen Hair." The character of this music is impressionistic. As in impressionistic painting there are no sharp, hard lines, so in impressionistic music the effects are subtle and atmospheric. Debussy's flaxen-haired girl is as different from Couperin's Soeur Monique as water lilies painted by Monet differ from the flowers that surround a Crivelli Madonna.

Therefore, the pianist in playing Debussy must release a different texture of sound—and that can only be done with a quite different feeling in the arms and hands and fingers.

The fingers will be kept rather flat. They will not *strike* the keys, but will cling to them as the arm draws the hand from place to place on the keyboard, following the contours of the melody. As one young student said: "It feels like drawing your hand through water, and watching the ripples that follow after you."

Since this piece is printed unfingered, it offers a wonderful opportunity for exploring the possibilities of fingering that will insure the continuous legato through which the music expresses itself. You can produce the sounds that the music calls for by letting the fingers follow the movement of the arm, often changing fingers on the same key, or sliding the same finger from one key to another.

Once you have made your fingering discoveries and have decided what fingers you will use, write them down in the music.

Parallel, Contrary, and Oblique Motions

Gesture can play an important part in expressing the direction of moving voices.

In music, two tones or groups of tones can move in relation to each other along three paths.

1) The tones can move in the same direction, both going up, or both going down. This is called *Parallel* motion. It is the quietest of the relationships in its effect on the ear — something like what we see when two actors on the stage move in the same direction. They may be side by side, or one may move faster or farther than the other. The gesture that you would make in parallel motion can be realized by holding both arms shoulder high in front of you, and moving them slowly to the right and then to the left, as you would move both arms either up or down the keyboard.

2) Much more energy is expressed if tones move in opposite directions, either going away from or approaching each other. This is called *Contrary* motion. Again, holding the arms out straight, spread them apart, moving them slowly away from each other. This gives a feeling in the body of width, of amplitude, perhaps of generosity. In music, when tones or chords move in this way, the aural effect is also one of amplitude. A very familiar example is the Authentic Cadence. In C major for instance, the leading tone B rises to C and the root G moves in contrary motion down to C.

Next, with the arms outstretched and far apart, move them slowly inward toward each other. In music when tones or chords move inward, they give the impression of closing in. A familiar example is the chord progression IV to V, where the upper voices move down against the ascending bass. The effect is the exact opposite of the contrary motion where the voices spread apart.

3) The last motion, *Oblique,* can be realized by holding each arm in turn straight out, while the other arm moves away from, then toward it. In music we can hear this effect when a tone or chord remains stationary, as in the Plagal Cadence: in C major, the keynote C in the IV chord is repeated in the I chord, while the other voices resolve downward in parallel motion to the tones of the tonic triad.

In the Chopin Prelude in C minor, Op. 28, No. 20, all three motions occur. Here is a simplified outline version of the first measure:

Play this illustration following the movement of the parts by letting
the upper arms travel freely right and left. Do this slowly and
softly, listening to the musical effect, while the tones move in contrary motion. Notice the effect of the contrasts in the *size* of the
intervals by which the voices move. In this measure, for example,
the treble travels only by seconds, covering the distance from A♭,
the highest note, down to E♭ below. But the bass proceeds by two
noble leaps: a descending fifth, C down to F, then an ascending fourth,
G up to C.

Here is the outline of the second line of the piece. The harmonic
mass of this line descends inexorably from the first chord to the last.

The melody is moving downward in two phrases; the first one
descends from E♭ down to G, the second from C down to C. However, in each phrase during its downward progress, the melody rises
for a poignant moment in contrary motion to the descending bass:
C rises to D, and E♭ rises to F. Each of these places is marked
in the illustration with an asterisk. It is as though, for an instant,
the melody glanced back up the sloping road it had traveled, then
resumed its inevitable downward march.

In playing this piece, the gesture of the upper arms should con-
form to the motion of the two contrasting melodic lines in treble
and bass. The slow and continuous movement of the music can
best be expressed if there is a slow and continuous movement of the
arms carrying the hands from chord to chord as the music travels
on its way.

Analyzing Similar Gestures in Parallel Passages

The introduction to the Chopin A-flat Polonaise, Op. 53, affords
an interesting study in gesture as applied to the playing of passages

that are similar musically and technically. This sixteen-measure introduction is based on a dominant pedal point and is a sort of glorifica-
tion of the tone E♭. As the music grows in intensity, these five
chords punctuate the upward progression, until it finally opens out
into the A-flat in which the Polonaise itself begins.

Play these chords in succession, as printed above. They are so
clearly related musically that you will probably use the same technical
gesture in playing each of them.

The chords are to be played *fortissimo,* as if by a full orchestra.
If you want a very brilliant tone with a touch of cymbal quality,
you will strike the keys from a distance. The hammers will hit the
strings quickly, and you will also hear the percussive sound of the
fingers striking the keys. If, however, you want a full but less brilliant
sound, you will touch the keys, and push the weight of your arm
and shoulder onto the fingertips. Try both ways, and decide which
tone quality you wish.

Now let us analyze the first eight measures of the introduction and
discuss the gestures to be used. The music consists of two 4-measure
phrases of similar construction. These similarities are identified in the
following illustration with letters A, B, C, D, and E.

A. The gesture to be employed with these chords has been discussed above.

B. Having decided on the fingering, play the two chromatic runs in succession. Be conscious of the gesture of the arms in parallel motion as they travel up the keyboard, bringing the hands abreast of each chord that the fingers must play. In making the crescendo, you can gradually add more arm weight, or more finger action, as the runs rush upward.

C. The upper arms will carry the hands swiftly and easily down to the chord C. In each phrase this chord is a reiteration of the harmony of the first chord of the phrase.

D. The upper arms will carry the hands to the right, until they are opposite the first of the two chords at D. Then, the arms moving inward in contrary motion will help in expressing the resolution of each seventh chord to the following triad.

E. Once more, the arms carry the hands down the keyboard. Work out, hands separately and then together, the contours and fingering of the repeated figures in sixteenth notes. In each phrase notice (that is, hear and feel) the relationship between the hands; the first two sixteenths are in similar motion and the last two in contrary motion. The music, beginning softly and growing in intensity, seems to bubble and boil like something seething in a huge cauldron, culminating in a crash (A).

After the related details of these two phrases have been studied in pairs this way, play the passage as written, remembering the *feel* of the sequence of the gestures that you have worked out.

There are innumerable instances in music where passages such as these can be "broken down" into their elements of related gesture, by playing in succession, out of context, chords or patterns that are musically related and that must feel technically alike to the performer.

Summary

Through you, music is expressed, that is, "pressed out." *Gesture* is one of the technical means at your disposal in this process of Ex-pression. Gesture is intrinsic. Its compulsion comes from within the music.

So, gesture is not an artificial affair, applied externally to your performance, like a kind of theatrical musical make-up. If gesture is superficial or exaggerated, if it is used to impress an audience with your own personality, if it is erratic and has degenerated into mannerisms, then it becomes a stumbling block which you erect, perhaps unconsciously, in the path of the free flow of the music.

In a class in Song Interpretation, the great teacher Povla Frijsh was listening to a young girl sing the amusing song of Chabrier, "Villanelle des Petits Canards." The student was singing with an exaggerated coyness and archness of expression and gesture that brought a look of astonishment to Mme. Frijsh's face. At the conclusion of the song, her first comment was, "My dear, we should never explain a joke! This song should be sung—what is the word you use?—deadpan!"

In my experience, if an interpretation *sounds* right, it will *feel* right in the arms and hands, and it will *look* right to the audience. A pianist or an instrumentalist is, in a way, an actor. He is conveying through the music, ideas he has not initially originated but which, through study, he has made his own.

An actor needs a wide vocabulary of gesture to give further meaning to the words that he speaks. And the pianist should learn that gesture gives further meaning to the music to be communicated to the audience. More important, it gives the music a chance to *sound* the way it is trying to, as the "imprisoned splendor" escapes.

Gesture, for every interpretative artist, should always be sincere and appropriate. A pianist once told me that he considered Gesture so important that even a deaf man watching an artist play should have some reasonable idea of what the music was conveying.

> Do not saw the air too much with your hand . . .
> But suit the action to the word. . . .

This is Hamlet's Advice to the Players. It is equally appropriate as Advice to Pianists. Suit the gesture to the music!

CONCLUSION

The only reason for learning to play the piano is to release music. Technique must always be regarded as a means to an end. Technique is for Music's sake.

The technical suggestions in this chapter are not given in order to make your hands and arms and fingers feel more comfortable, per se, although this will probably take place. The whole point is that these suggestions may help you to help the music be itself. Your attention should always be focused on the sounds you are making. Listen, and listen, and listen unremittingly!

When I suggest that if you move your upper arm, you can get quickly and surely from one place on the keyboard to another, or that if your hand is far back on the keys, your fingers can reach keys that might otherwise be difficult to touch, I do not mean that acquiring these skills is an end in itself. High knuckles, low knuckles, light arm, heavy arm, finger stroke, arm weight, curved fingers, flat fingers, let the elbow lead, rotate the arm—use any of these ways of playing, or any other means that you know, if they help you to produce the sounds that—as far as you understand—express the music. So, if in one way you cannot make the sounds you want, try another way. Technique is best acquired by experimentation and the investigation of your own physical resources.

In this chapter I have tried to suggest a point of view that may be of use to you in your piano study. This point of view is perfectly expressed by Emerson in his essay on *Literary Ethics,* where he says, "Explore, and explore. Be neither chided nor flattered out of your position of perpetual inquiry."

Part IV. Pupils' Recitals and the Spring Concert

THE "SATURDAY MORNING CONCERTS"

Many teachers have their students play for each other at frequent informal recitals in their own studios during the teaching season. In addition, many teachers have a Spring Concert, which is a formal affair, and is probably held in a larger place.

Building an interesting program for either of these types of recital is a challenge to the teacher's imagination and ingenuity. A Pupil's Recital often is an occasion that creates nervous tension on the part of all concerned: pupils, teachers, and audience. But it can be a pleasurable experience for everyone if the program is well planned and if a friendly, musical atmosphere is established.

Music is a social art, and a student who is used to playing at home for his family and friends will be at ease in playing for others anywhere. Playing before an audience will not be an unusual or terrifying experience for him. His attitude, formed in the early years, will be determined largely by the point of view of his teacher and his parents. If they are wise, he will realize that it is the *music* and not he himself as the performer that is important.

I would like to give an account of how a series of informal recitals was conducted in a Music School with which I was connected for many years. The recitals described here were given by children and young people in the Junior Department. Their ages were from six to sixteen. Each pupil played three times during the year in the series of "Saturday Morning Concerts."

The audience was composed mainly of mothers, with a sprinkling of fathers and some of the older students. However, on one occasion a small boy at his first appearance produced two parents, a grand-

131

mother, a sister, two cousins, and an aunt! When introductions were made after the concert, it sounded as though they had all arrived from "H.M.S. Pinafore"!

In their weekly classes in musicianship, the pupils had frequently played and discussed the pieces they had learned in their individual piano lessons.

At the Saturday Morning Concerts the performers were expected to stay until the end of the program. We discouraged the request, occasionally made by a parent: "Please let Susie play first, so that I can take her to the dentist," or "the dancing class," or whatever the next engagement might be in the New York child's busy Saturday.

We wanted both Susie and her mother to feel that playing a piece on Saturday morning was not merely meeting a School obligation. Neither was it taking a musical examination to see whether Susie could play her piece or not. Rather, her piece was an integral part of a complete program, and hearing the entire program was the musical experience we wished them both to have.

SECURING VARIETY IN THE PROGRAMS

These Saturday Morning Concerts lasted a little over an hour, with fifteen to twenty pupils playing each week. The concerts usually began with a familiar song played by one of the pupils, and sung by everyone, including the audience. A special favorite was our own School song, "We Thy People Praise Thee." The tune is the St. Anthony Chorale by Haydn, with words written by Kate Stearns Page. Other songs were sometimes interspersed between the piano numbers. And at Christmas time, several pupils played Christmas carols, which everyone sang.

Pupils of all ages and varying degrees of pianistic proficiency took part in each program, and this was a valuable experience for everyone. The younger pupils were hearing music the older ones played, which they too would some day be playing; and the older pupils had the satisfaction of hearing the easier pieces that they once had played, and could realize how far they themselves had progressed.

We have all sat through programs where, as the performers were successively older and older, the pieces were longer and longer, ending perhaps with the Best Pupil playing a concerto. Such a program arrangement is a test of endurance for the pupils, as it surely is for the audience. To avoid this, at the Saturday Morning Concerts the little children's pieces were not all played at the beginning but were distributed throughout the program. After listening, perhaps, to an older pupil play a movement of a Beethoven sonata, it was a pleasant change to see and hear a smaller pianist perform "The Happy Farmer."

Since boys were fewer than girls, the boys were spaced thriftily throughout the program. Duets and other ensemble numbers were played between the solo pieces. We made a point of having children in the same family play duets, wherever this could be accomplished without too much friction in practicing together at home. Sometimes an older brother or sister who played the violin would contribute a number, accompanied by a young pianist.

Sometimes the program included a brief demonstration of class work in Keyboard Harmony, or Ear Training of one kind or another. Sometimes an original composition would be played. Sometimes, if a pupil extemporized easily, we would play an unrehearsed game called "Snatch as Snatch Can." The pupil and I would sit side by side at the piano. I would improvise a phrase of music, and the pupil would improvise an answering phrase. We would continue this antiphonal extemporization until we had "made up" a fairly respectable piece together.

On one program, a group of Sixth Grade pupils gave a brief description of the Beethoven Fifth Symphony, which they had been studying in Musicianship. In the class they had heard the symphony on phonograph records, and had studied the music first with the piano score, and later with the orchestral score. One pupil spoke briefly of Beethoven; another described Symphonic Form. Then several pupils played in turn the themes of this symphony.

On another occasion, some of the children performed an arrangement that I had made of the "Story of Siegfried." One pupil read the narrative, which was illustrated by twenty themes that had been assigned to as many children of all ages. The themes varied in difficulty from the "Dragon Motive," which crawled around realistically as played by a small beginner, to the "Magic Fire Scene" and "The Awakening of Brünnhilde," played by older pupils. The group of children stood quietly at one side of the piano; before the reader began the narrative, the child who was to play the first theme had taken her place on the piano bench, ready to play when the time came, the "Nature Motive," where the River Rhine rolls along. As soon as she had played her theme, and while the continuing narrative was being read, she slipped quietly back into the group of standing children, and the child who was to play next as quietly took her place, ready to play the second theme, where Mime taps his hammer and hops over the ground. This procedure continued during the 20 minutes in which the story was unfolding. The last theme was played by a small boy who could not reach the pedal if he sat on the bench. So he stood in front of the piano, and brought the performance to a close as, with a magnificent flourish, he played the "Sword Motive."

In no case did the children give the impression that they were soloists. They were simply a group of young Wagnerian enthusiasts, telling an interesting story in words and music.

Later in the season many of the children heard a performance of "Siegfried" at the Metropolitan Opera House, and were especially delighted to recognize their own themes as they occurred in the opera.

ORGANIZING AND WRITING EACH PROGRAM

For these informal concerts we had no printed programs. Since the pieces to be played might range from "Lavender's Blue" to a concerto movement, the problem was to arrange the pieces in groups so that the program would hold together.

At the commencement of the concert, I wrote group headings on the blackboard. They might be: Folk Music, Dances, Descriptive Music, etc. This gave plenty of latitude, since Dance Music might include both a Handel minuet and a Chopin waltz, and Descriptive Music might run from "The Wild Horseman" to "Clair de Lune."

I asked each child to tell me in which category he thought his piece should come, and sometimes we found that we had to add the slightly ambiguous heading "Miscellaneous."

The names of the pieces themselves were not written on the blackboard, only the group headings. But we had one special column headed "V.I.P." Under this I wrote, at the children's dictation, a chronological list of the names of the great composers whose music was to be played that morning. At times there were amusing discussions as to who was, and who wasn't, a Very Important Person! A child who played the Heller "Avalanche" would say that the piece belonged to the Descriptive Music group, but would insist that Heller be listed as a V.I.P. And another child, who was going to play a piece written by his teacher, saw no reason for not including the teacher's name in the column along with Bach and Mozart. Pieces by V.I.P.'s that had not been placed in any of the categories usually came under the heading "Various Pieces by Great Composers."

TWO SPECIMEN PROGRAMS

The following are two specimen programs of pieces that were played at these Saturday Morning Concerts:

PROGRAM No. I

1. *Song*
   We Thy People Praise Thee ....Haydn
2. *Folk Music*
   Charlie is My Darlin' — (Duet) ....Scottish
   Come, Sweet Lass ....English
   Sur le Pont d'Avignon ....French
   The Disagreeable Lover ....Russian
   Come Away! Come Away! — (Duet) ....Swabian
3. *Dances*
   Waltz in E minor ....Grieg
   Fantastic Dance No. 1 ....Shostakovich
   Minuet in G minor ....Bach
   Minuet in G major ....Mozart
   Minuet in G ....Beethoven
4. *Various Pieces by Great Composers*
   Prelude in C major ....Bach
   Musette ....Bach
   Sicilienne — (Two Pianos) ....Bach
   Grillen ....Schumann
   Soldiers' March ....Schumann
   Piano Concerto in B-flat, Last Movement (Two Pianos)....Mozart

The V.I.P.'s on the above program were, of course:

> Bach
> Haydn
> Mozart
> Beethoven
> Schumann

Grieg and Shostakovich were in the "Doubtful" column.

PROGRAM No. II

1. *Song*
   Glory, Glory, Hallelujah!
2. *Descriptive Music*
   Hunting Song ....John Davenport
   Hunting Song ....Grovlez
   Summer Idyl ....Frederic Hart
   Run, Run ....Pinto
   Bogey-Man ....Gail Welles
   Golliwog's Cake-Walk ....Debussy
3. *Sonata Movements*
   Sonatina in G major, First Movement ....Clementi
   Sonatina in F major, First Movement ....Beethoven
   Sonata in D major, Finale ....Haydn

4. *Various Pieces by Great Composers*
    Invention in D minor ....Bach
    Variations in C major ....Beethoven
    Waltz in C-sharp minor ....Chopin
    Prelude in C minor ....Chopin
    Mazurka in A minor ....Chopin

The V.I.P.'s here were undoubtedly:
    Bach
    Haydn
    Beethoven
    Chopin
    Debussy

RUNNING THE PERFORMANCE

The pupils who were going to perform at the concert sat in three rows, facing the platform, with the audience seated behind them. I occupied an inconspicuous chair on one side of the platform. I had, of course, a list of the pupils who were to play, and the names of their pieces. The performers, however, did not know the order in which they were to play, though I had previously planned this to give unity as well as variety to the program. As the program went along, I announced the name of the pupil who would play next, and he or she would mount the platform.

Getting Started

Since pupils of all sizes and all lengths of legs were to play on the same program, the first thing that each one did before playing was to adjust the stool to the correct height for himself. A young performer whose feet could not reach the floor would, in addition, get a footstool to put them on, in order to sit comfortably. It was hoped that the children would make similar preparations at home before practicing. (Telephone books, as long as they last, make excellent footstools!)

These preliminaries being over, the pupil would announce what he was going to play, giving the name of the piece, the composer, and sometimes adding any information about the piece that he thought would interest the audience. On one occasion a child announced:

> I am going to play the "Solfeggietto" by C. P. E. Bach. He was the third son of John Sebastian Bach. In this piece, the same tune comes three different times in different keys.

In order to keep a pupil from rushing into playing his piece the moment he sat down, and from dashing off the platform at its conclusion, taking the last note with him, we tried to establish a routine of calmness. The pupil (usually!) sat quietly at the piano for a moment with his hands in his lap, going over in his mind the first phrase that he was going to play. At the conclusion of the piece, before arising, he listened to the last sounds that he had played. This routine set each piece within a "Frame of Silence," and helped to establish an easy and unhurried atmosphere for both performers and audience.

Listening as Well as Playing

These recitals had two objects. One was to have the pupils play pieces, and the second was to have them *listen* with appreciation and discrimination to music that other people played. The Saturday Morning Concerts gave an excellent opportunity for "learning to listen."

Since phrasing in music, as in any other language, is the principal element in conveying meaning, we wanted the pupils always to hear the phrasing accurately in other people's playing as well as in their own. Children's ears are usually so sensitive that with training they can hear inaccurate musical phrasing as easily as they can hear mispronounced words in English.

Though we often discussed the structure or content of the pieces, I usually discouraged criticism of the playing. But once, after a student had given a brilliant performance of the Schubert E-flat major Impromptu, but had played it far too fast, I asked for comments "from the floor" and said, "Has anyone anything to say about how the Impromptu sounded?" One pupil volunteered: "It couldn't go like *that!*" Another one said, "She plays it very well, but she went so fast that you couldn't hear the phrasing." And a small boy commented dourly, "No expression!"

A-B-A Form: Long and Short Pieces

Of course, in every program some of the pieces were short and others were longer. The problem was two-fold: to make the smaller pieces sound as attractive as possible, and to see to it that the younger children were attentive while the longer pieces were being played.

The situation was often enlivened for a young beginner if he played his piece twice. He would play it alone, and then repeat it while I played an accompaniment on a second piano. A little folk-tune that seems insignificant when played alone may sound quite impressive if an accompaniment is added.

In order to hold the attention of the younger children, I tried various devices. The children had studied the structure of the pieces they played themselves, and were interested in recognizing these elements of structure in the pieces that other people played.

For instance, most of the pupils were familiar with A-B-A form. So if a piece in this form was to be played, I sometimes asked the pupils to rise quietly when the B part commenced, and so sit down as noiselessly when the A part reappeared. In order to avoid the sound of scuffling feet, the pupils practiced rising and sitting down silently. They were asked to sit on the front edge of the chairs with their weight well forward and their feet planted squarely on the floor. Then, at the exact moment, they all rose without the sound of a single scraping foot, then sat down again as noiselessly. (Incidentally, this bit of technique is recommended for the standing up and sitting down of choirs and choruses.)

If a piece such as a sonata movement was to be played, I would tell the children that it was going to be long, and that they must sit quietly. In order to hold their interest, the soloist would first play the principal themes of the movement, and the other children would be asked to listen for their appearance in the performance. I suggested that each child choose a comfortable position before the piece was played, and stay that way until the end of the piece.

Stretch and Change Seats

Near the middle of the program I would suggest that all the pupils stand up and stretch, as is done at the seventh inning in a baseball game. And, in order to "change the vibrations," I would ask them to exchange seats, two at a time, until everyone had a new neighbor. (This is an idea that many of us might consider a pleasant innovation at some of the concerts that *we* attend!)

REPORT ON THE PERFORMANCE: THE TEACHERS' BULLETIN BOARD

After each concert, I dictated a somewhat detailed report on the pupils' playing. This was typed and put on the Bulletin Board in the office of the School, where it was read by the piano teachers of the pupils who had played that morning. (The children, of course, did not see the board.) The report was usually followed up by talks with the teachers about the pupils and their progress.

The Bulletin Board was also part of an interdepartmental communication system. For instance, a piano teacher might write a note to a class teacher:

> Jimmie W. is going to study the Schumann "Soldiers' March."
>
> He has not learned
>
> Can you take it up in class?

Or a class teacher might write to a piano teacher:

> Marjorie R. played "May Night" in class very musically. But she played several measures in 6 meter, with two beats to the measure,
> $$\frac{6}{4}$$
> losing the effect of syncopation.
>
> Isn't the whole piece 3 meter, and counted "Two-Three-One"?
> $$\frac{3}{2}$$
> Can you help? Perhaps she could play it again in class sometime?

Concert reports and the exchange of notes between the teachers helped in securing that correlation of the work between the departments that is so necessary in any school.

ANOTHER TYPE OF PROGRAM

In the foregoing informal concert programs, piano playing was the important feature. But in the program described here, Musicianship and Piano Playing shared equally.

This program was given by four children at the end of twenty weeks of music study. Tony had had some lessons the previous winter. The other three were beginners. The little girls, Catherine and Riki, were seven years old. The boys were older — Scooter was ten and Tony eleven. Every week each of them had an individual piano lesson, and each pair also had a weekly class lesson in musicianship. Because of many outside interests their practicing was rather sketchy, though they learned a great deal at the lessons. All four children were unusually intelligent. And the winter's work gave them a good start and an interest in music itself, which was a solid basis for their further study.

At this concert, the audience consisted of the children's parents, some friends, and a number of teachers from the college with which the children's fathers were connected.

The audience entered by a door that opened directly into the studio. In order that latecomers should not come bursting in when the children were playing, I asked Tony, who was fond of printing, if he would make a sign to hang on the door. I suggested that the sign might say, "The Concert has begun. Please come in the back way." He said, "Yes, or we *might* say, 'The concert has commenced. Please enter at rear door.' " Using this Chesterfieldian English, he produced a handsome sign, decorated with pink roses, a pattern of sixteenth notes, and a scroll of music. Latecomers entered via the kitchen!

Each of the audience was given a copy of the following program:

SEASON 1951 - 52

THIRD CONCERT

March 30, 1952

Given by

Catherine White	Riki Diller
Scooter White	Tony Diller

PROGRAM

1. *Song*
   My Country, 'Tis of Thee   Scooter

140

2. *Duets*

Happy Birthday to You ⎫
Counting Out   ⎬   Catherine and Scooter
The Old Soldier   ⎭

Sulky Sue   ⎫
Queen Caroline   ⎬   Riki and Tony
Happy Birthday to You   ⎭

3. *Solos* (Rote Pieces Dedicated to the Performers by A.D.)

Cradle Song   Catherine
Hop, Skip, Jump!   Riki
Bogey-Man   Scooter
In a Chinese Theater   Tony

4. *Class Work in Musicianship: The Materials of Musical Composition*

1. Major Scales in Tetrachords   Catherine
2. All Triads in C Major   Riki
3. Sound: Piano Action   Tony
4. Overtones and Sympathetic Vibration   Tony and Scooter
5. Major Triad in 6 Shapes   Tony and Scooter
6. Tonal Magnetism   Tony and Scooter
7. Five and Seven-Note Tunes   Tony
8. Harmonizing a Tone in 7 Major Keys   Tony and Scooter
9. Scale-Step Names   Scooter
10. Chain Questions   Everybody
11. Major and Relative Minor   Scooter and Tony
12. Cadences: Authentic, Plagal, and Complete Scooter
    Half, Deceptive, and Delayed   Tony
13. French Time Names   Scooter and Tony
14. Sequences   Scooter and Tony
15. Universal Modulation   Scooter and Tony

5. *Solos*

Hot Cross Buns   ⎫
The King of France   ⎬   Riki

Our Defenders   ⎫
Katydid   ⎬   Catherine

A Young Lady Named Lent   Scooter

Reverie   ⎫
Russian Dance   ⎬   Tony

6. *Duets*

Susan Mills   Tony and Scooter
The Lincolnshire Poacher

Augustin   Riki and Catherine

7. *Song*

The Star-Spangled Banner   Tony

For the first number the audience rose and sang "My Country, 'Tis of Thee." Then came some "family duets," each brother and sister playing together. Every family should be able to play "Happy Birthday to You," so it appeared twice. The duets had words which the little girls recited, clapping the time-values, before the pieces were played.

The duets were followed by a group of solos that had been learned by rote. The children had not seen the printed music, and the pieces were more showy than those that they could read. In learning them, we had discussed the structure of the pieces, and I taught them by rote directly on the keyboard.

Next came a demonstration of class work in the materials of musical composition. The boys, especially, were far more interested in the structure of music than they were in practicing pieces, and had spent much time at the piano "investigating" and "composing." So they demonstrated with enthusiasm such matters as overtones, tonal magnetism, cadences, and modulation.

Their original Chain Question was amusing. In a Chain Question each answer becomes the beginning of the next question. For example:

"Start on G. What is the Dominant?" .... D
"Go up a Major Third" .... F#
"That is 2 of what Major Scale?" .... E
"What is its Relative Minor?" .... C#

I improvised several Chain Questions like the above, which they answered correctly. I had asked them previously if they would like to make up a Chain Question for me to answer. They had a wonderful time! They had written a chain of 15 items in the most outrageous keys. They asked the questions antiphonally, and said that I must keep the answers in my head, giving only the final one. At the end of the long series Tony said, "You may tell the answer now." I ventured, "B major?" "That is correct," said Tony. But Scooter interrupted, "There's one more. What is a chromatic half-step above the leading tone of the relative minor?" The answer is F-triple sharp, which I obligingly missed, to their great delight.

After this came more solos and duets. For the last number the audience rose and sang "The Star-Spangled Banner."

At the conclusion of the concert, the audience drank tea, and the performers ate ice cream. Adults and children agreed that "a pleasant time was had by all!"

THE SPRING CONCERT

With the coming of June the teaching season reaches its apotheosis. All over the land hundreds of teachers and pupils brace themselves for the consummation of their winter's work — the grand finale of the season — the Spring Concert.

This is too frequently an occasion involving nervous tension, best clothes, rented chairs, and long, hard pieces. Some teachers, perhaps remembering their participation in Spring Concerts in their own youth, do not include this event at the season's end.

One ingenuous young woman who was just beginning her teaching career was discussing her future plans with me. She described the kind of music teaching that she wanted to do, and ended with: "But I shall *never* have a Spring Concert! It spoils everything! Is it true that all teachers begin thinking about the Spring Concert in August, and hand out the pieces the first of September? I don't think that's the way to do it, to drill your pupils on one piece all year. The idea, I suppose, is to have them play their pieces until they know them, but if they practice them a whole winter, the pieces will be stale by the time spring comes, won't they?"

I assured her that they would. But I told her that the Spring Concert is traditional in most communities, and that many parents and children look upon it as a gala occasion at the end of the season. It is in the same class as Promotion Day exercises in school. I also told her that if she could arrange an interesting and varied program, which was not made exclusively of pieces that had been practiced so long that they were shopworn, the Spring Concert could be a pleasant occasion.

Suggestions as to Program

Most of the suggestions given earlier in this Part as to organizing the programs of informal Pupils' Recitals can be used to advantage in preparing the program for the Spring Concert.

Ideally, the parents and friends of the performers have come to the Spring Concert to hear some music, as well as to hear certain students play and sing. Establishing a cordial rapport between the audience and performers is essential.

143

Everybody Sing

As in the formal recital, an excellent way of achieving this is to begin the program with the audience on its feet, singing together, while a student accompanies at the piano. They will then be in a more receptive mood to hear music than if, up to the last minute, they had been reading the program to discover when Rosalind and Peter were going to play, or to calculate hopefully when the concert would be over!

It is wonderful how quickly an audience can be brought together through the musical experience of community singing. The Spring Concert that begins with audience and performers singing, for example, "The Ode to Joy" or "America, the Beautiful" is certainly off to a good start!

Avoid Too Long a Program

Even the hardiest parents and most devoted friends cannot be expected to keep interested in hearing pupils play for more than an hour and a half. It is obvious that concerts should not be too long, and should begin when scheduled and end promptly.

Avoid Very Long Pieces

An audience will probably listen more appreciatively to two fairly short pieces in contrasted style than to one very long piece. For example, "Des Abends" and "Aufschwung" played by a student make a more interesting number on the program than, perhaps, a performance of a piece like the Handel "Passacaglia," with all the repeats!

The Parents' Attitude

Much of the success of the Spring Concert depends on the attitude of the pupils' parents and the teacher, both before and during the concert.

Parents can have a part in making the concert a success by helping their children to keep calm and to think of the performance as an opportunity of sharing music with a friendly audience. I would avoid last-minute fussing with the children's appearance — twitching neckties and putting hair ribbons in place. It is better for a boy to play with musical feeling, even if his necktie is under one ear, than for him to have so much of his attention on his necktie that he has none left for the music he is playing.

I remember one occasion when a young student overcame excellently the handicap of a too solicitous parent. Our School was giving a Spring Concert at Town Hall in New York. Phyllis, a thirteen-year-old pupil, was going to play the Bach A minor English Suite. She journeyed downtown with her mother and an aunt, who told me afterwards of the conversation that had been going on as they approached the concert hall.

The mother kept reiterating, "Now, Phyllis, don't be nervous! You know you've practiced your piece, and you're not going to forget it!"

Phyllis, who possessed great concentration and had lived for thirteen years with this parent, replied: "I'm not nervous. Yes, I have, and I hope I won't!"

Phyllis was quite accustomed to playing for an audience, since she had played frequently at our Saturday Morning Concerts. She was musical, and was used to keeping her head, so the Suite went very well.

At the end of the concert, her mother embraced her, moist-eyed with relief, and said within my own hearing: "Oh, Phyllis darling, you played beautifully! *Weren't you nervous?*" And Phyllis replied, "No. There was so much to think about, that I couldn't be!"

The Teacher's Attitude

Much of the atmosphere of a Spring Concert can be created by the teacher's attitude while the playing is going on.

If she sits on the edge of her chair and follows every note with apparent anxiety, this nervousness will be contagious. If the pieces are not going well, she may look as though she were saying to herself: "Adele forgot to make the crescendo that we worked over so long in the Chopin étude. She can play it much better than that!" Or, "Frank is keeping his foot on the soft pedal all the way through. He never did that in his life before!"

But, on the other hand, if the teacher can be interested and relaxed, and look as if she were enjoying the music that is being played, her sense of ease and appreciation will be communicated to everyone, and all will be well.

Advice to a Pupil

Years ago, when I was a young student, I had a wise teacher, Alice Fowler, who gave me some excellent advice about playing in public, which I have never forgotten.

At my last lesson before one concert she said to me: "You have worked hard and you know your pieces. You have played them very well, so there is nothing more we can do about that! Get plenty of sleep. The night before the concert go to bed early. The next day take a walk. Practice two or three hours on anything you like, but don't play these pieces over and over. Because if you play them badly, you will worry; and if they go well, you may feel cocky, and lose your concentration. In either event they will 'go stale,' and at the concert your pieces should sound as fresh to you as to the audience. Think about the music you are going to play. Above all, *feel musical* and Bach and Chopin will probably 'come through'."

Conclusion

If the program is varied and interesting, if the teacher is relaxed and unapprehensive, if the students have prepared their pieces well, the audience will be friendly and attentive. The coincidence of all these factors will surely make the Spring Concert an occasion that everyone will enjoy and remember as a happy musical experience.

Part V. What Parents Can Do

Introduction

Fortunate is the child who is born into a musical family: not necessarily one in which the parents are professional musicians, but a family where music is a usual and expected part of home life, which everyone shares, and to which everyone contributes. There are many homes in which parents make music a family affair, like riding or sailing, or any of the other activities in which children are eager to participate with their parents.

The parents of children who are especially talented have a unique responsibility. These children often show precocious musical and technical gifts at a very early age. It is the parents' and teachers' business to nurture these gifts, and these children obviously should have special training. But one of the saddest things that can happen to a musically gifted child is exploitation by the parent or the teacher, either for glory or for financial gain. This may hamper the child's development as a normal human being. "Child prodigies," however, are numerically few, and this chapter has to do with the parents of children of average musical gifts.

I believe that all children are innately musical, and all children should be given a musical education, beginning in the kindergarten. We know that all normal children, not only the especially gifted, can learn to read English. Mother Stevens, the head of the Pius X School of Liturgical Music at the Convent of the Sacred Heart in New York, went so far as to say that with intelligent teaching every normal child can learn to read vocal music at sight.

If a child expresses a definite desire to play an instrument, I think a year or more of the piano furnishes the best groundwork for the study of any instrument. The first piano work can begin at the age of seven or eight.

In my own experience of teaching a great many children to play the piano, several, of course, changed to other instruments after a year or two. But I remember only three children who I felt should not

147

continue music lessons at all. One was a young girl with a gift for drawing and painting, who did not have any time to spend on music. Another was a boy with a strong scientific bent, who was frankly not interested in the sound of music. And the third was a recalcitrant small boy who didn't want to spend any time on anything that anyone wanted him to do!

In piano study, parents, teachers, and pupils all play important roles. Ways in which Parents can be particularly helpful are described in this Part.

MUSIC IN THE HOME

The Child's Contribution

If a child is taking piano lessons, his parents can be helpful by encouraging him to play for the family the pieces he has been studying. Both parents and children should feel that music lessons are very special. For instance, Johnny's report card from school may show that he got an A or a B in spelling or arithmetic, and that is the end of the matter. But if Johnny has learned a new piece, he should feel that he has a contribution to make to the social life of the family. He should play willingly at any time when asked to do so.

The choice of *what* he plays should be left to the teacher, who will discuss with him at his lesson just which pieces are "finished." The attitude of the parents can be most helpful if they show real interest in the child's "old pieces." Otherwise, when he is asked to play for the family, he may try to perform the first part of the new piece that he began to learn last Wednesday. If Johnny feels that he must produce something new every time he is asked to play, tell him that every artist plays the same pieces over and over. Paderewski probably played the Waldstein Sonata hundreds of times in as many concerts.

Parents do not have to be especially musical in order to take an intelligent interest in the music their children play. But they can at least know the names of the pieces the child has studied. For example, requests like the following will be encouraging: "Will you play the Beethoven Sonatina for us?" Or, "We haven't heard the Chopin Prelude for a long time. Won't you play it?" Or, "Do you remember the Brahms Waltzes?" And after the performance, the comment might be something like, "That was a lovely piece. Thank you" — rather than "You played [or "You didn't play"] very well."

Children's playing should be listened to with respectful attention, since it is the music, as well as the child, that is being heard.

This was beautifully illustrated one day when I was calling on friends who have a large family of children. Both parents are excellent musicians. The room was filled with adults, children, and dogs. I was playing a game with one of the little girls, when suddenly she looked up and said, "We must stop now. Jonathan [her younger brother, aged eight] is going to play the recorder." He played several old English melodies charmingly, while his mother accompanied him at the piano. Even the dogs quieted down, and we all listened as attentively as though we were hearing Heifetz play a Bach Violin Sonata at Carnegie Hall.

Ensemble Playing

The child's contribution to music in the home need not be confined to playing the pieces he has studied. The teacher should discover as soon as possible what the family musical situation is. Does any other member of the family play an instrument? If Mother used to play the violin but "gave up her music when she married," she should be encouraged to get out her instrument and play something that her child can accompany on the piano. And if Father once studied the piano, he might revive the accomplishment and play duets with his children.

Playing on rhythm band instruments can furnish an entertaining half hour of informal musical ensemble for the family and friends. Many collections of rhythm band music are published, where the piano gives the musical background, and the triangle, tambourine, drum, and cymbals supply the rhythmic accompaniment. These four instruments are not kindergarten toys, but are the instruments used, for example, by Beethoven in the "Turkish music" in the last movement of the Ninth Symphony.

A collection of folk songs is published with words that can be sung by a group, while the rhythm instruments play a discreet accompaniment. There is also an excellent collection of piano pieces by Schubert, arranged with rhythm band accompaniment. These two collections are printed with the percussion parts written out, so that they can be read like the parts of any orchestral score. The Toy Symphony attributed to Haydn is another work with easy instrumental parts, which is fun for a group of amateurs to play.

Recorder playing offers another opportunity for ensemble music in the home. The recorder is steadily growing in popularity, and it is not difficult for an interested parent to learn to play tunes on this instrument. In many schools recorder playing is part of the regular curriculum, and recorders are not expensive. The collections of music for two, three, and four recorders can give the family the opportunity of playing music in parts. Then there is a wealth of 18th-century music that is not technically difficult, but is written for various combinations of recorders and piano. This may open the door to a world of chamber music literature, and may lead later on to that most delightful form of ensemble playing, the string quartet.

Family Singing

Group singing is perhaps the happiest and easiest way in which the family can make music together. Everybody is invited to participate, and no practice is necessary! All that is needed is enthusiastic parents who will get the family together to sing.

The teacher can cooperate by helping Johnny to learn to play the piano accompaniments. This will give an added interest to his piano lessons. He may learn some familiar songs, hymns, and Christmas carols. For family celebrations, I would suggest that every young student learn to play "Happy Birthday to You." Johnny might learn to play his father's college song — perhaps it will be "Fair Harvard" or "Boola, Boola." And on Thanksgiving Day, he can play the Netherlands hymn "We gather together to ask the Lord's blessing," which the family can sing before Father carves the turkey.

The repertory might also include patriotic songs: "My Country, 'Tis of Thee," or "America, the Beautiful," or "The Star-Spangled Banner." (This last should be played in a low key, preferably G major, so that "the rockets' red glare" can be sung comfortably by the parents, if Mother is not a high soprano, or Father a lyric tenor!)

A generation ago when Gilbert and Sullivan comic operas were the vogue, many happy evenings were spent with everyone gathered around the piano, singing the familiar music. The scores of "H. M. S. Pinafore" and "The Mikado" were on many a piano music rack. Little Buttercup and Koko were intimates in the family circle. The tunes were easy enough for a young student to play, and the delight of this "Hausmusik" lingers in the memory of many of us.

Nowadays Johnny may want to learn easy arrangements of some of the delightful Rodgers and Hammerstein songs. Singing "Oh, What a Beautiful Morning!" can be a cheerful experience at any hour of the day or night.

In time, the family may venture into singing music in parts. There is a wealth of choral literature that is exciting to explore and is not too difficult for amateur singers. Making music together is contagious, and family singing has often expanded into the organization of a neighborhood chorus where Bach chorales, or part songs of Mendelssohn or Schubert or Brahms are studied.

"Classical" and "Popular"

Nowadays our ears are filled with innumerable "Song Hits." Some of them are bound to be short-lived; others will live longer. Time alone will tell. But if the members of the family are interested in singing these songs, Johnny's teacher will probably cooperate gladly, and will help him to learn to play some of them.

Because he plays with enthusiasm the music from the latest "Hit Parade," it does not follow that he will cease to be interested in the Mozart sonata that he is studying.

It seems to me that there should not be a hard and fast dividing line between "high-brow" and "low-brow" music. There is really no quarrel between "popular" and "classical." I did not always realize this, and I remember an instance in my very early teaching career when I "taught classical" exclusively. I might have saved the situation for one pupil had I been wiser. I was teaching a girl of sixteen, who played quite well and was really interested in Bach and Schumann. One day, however, her mother came to me and began: "I don't care much for all this classical music that Lily plays. Can't you give her something else?"

I asked, "What music would you like her to play?" I remember verbatim her reply: "Oh, when we have company for dinner, afterwards I'd like Lily to go over to the piano, run her hands over the keys, and dash into something popular."

I felt so inadequate in this situation that the lessons were stopped by mutual consent. Now, however, I realize that I might have injected something "popular" in Lily's repertory without sacrificing the "classical" literature that she loved, and that I knew she should be studying.

Of course, there is much so-called "classical" music that is extremely dull, and much "popular" music that is well-written. Fifteen-year-old Cecilia had a good answer when someone asked her if she liked "jazz." She replied, "Sure, I do, just as I do ice cream sodas, but not to live on!"

Using What You Have in the House

Imperious Caesar dead and turned to clay
May stop a hole to keep the wind away.

I am not in favor of what we sometimes hear on the radio, where great music is made to serve commercial ends, and a theme from a symphony becomes identified with a breakfast food or the newest detergent. I regret the close association of William Tell and the Lone Ranger. However, it is sometimes necessary to use what music you have at your command.

The following incident illustrates this point. Margaret, aged ten, had a birthday party. I met her afterwards, and asked who came and what games they played. She gave me details, ending with "Harry played for Musical Chairs." Since Harry was a little beginner and a pupil of mine whose repertory was limited to three pieces, I asked what he had played. She replied, "Mostly that Minuet that he does!" I hope that Mozart will forgive this stop-and-go use that was made of his charming little piece!

LISTENING TO RECORDS
Record Collecting

Many parents are record collectors. This is a delightful hobby. Listening to beautiful records is a fine cultural experience for children as well as for adults.

With the advent of television and the great increase of music programs heard on the radio, many people have felt that the record industry was on the way out. Happily, quite the opposite has occurred. On both television and radio you can hear only the scheduled programs, but with your own records you can play your favorite pieces over and over again.

Older pupils can be encouraged to make their own collections. Records make wonderful Christmas presents! I know of two teen-age boys who were given recordings of the Beethoven Fifth Symphony. One had Toscanini's recording and the other had Bruno Walter's. They discussed the differences of interpretation with as much interest as though they were discussing the performances of two baseball teams.

Children who have heard good music when they are young will have a background of musical experience that will stand them in good stead all of their lives. Of course, children may not *understand* much of what they hear, but the musical impressions will be made. Similarly, when fine literature is read to children, they may not understand a great deal of it, but they will realize that they are in the presence of something on a large scale.

Many lists of recommended records are published. Here is my own short list of "Musts" for the nucleus of a collection of symphonic music for parents and older children.

> Haydn — "Surprise" Symphony
> Haydn — "Clock" Symphony
> Mozart — G minor Symphony
> Beethoven — Fifth Symphony
> Schubert — "Unfinished" Symphony
> Dvořák — "New World" Symphony

It should be stimulating to a young student to follow the piano score of the music while the records are being played, and it will help him in his sight reading. The piano scores of the symphonies listed above are printed in arrangements by Percy Goetschius in his Analytical Series published by Ditson. The music is clearly printed, and there are many indications of the structure. The themes are identified, and the phrasing is made very clear, so the music is quite easy to follow.

The piano teacher can show the pupil how to "keep the place" while following the piano score. Later on, he may perhaps be interested in following the orchestral score itself.

About Eleanor

There is as great a diversity of parents as there is of records. But ten-year-old Eleanor was most fortunate in her choice of a record-playing father. She was an unusually friendly little girl and was most talkative at her first lesson.

She played the Bach G major Minuet, and when she finished she said, "I know a lot about Bach." I asked where she got her information. She replied, "Daddy tells me about all the composers. Bach had twenty children and he played the organ. When he was an old man he was blind because, when he was a little boy, he copied too much music by moonlight." I asked what kind of music Bach wrote. She answered "He wrote all different kinds. He wrote my Minuet and the Passionate St. John." This last was so startling that I asked her to repeat it. "Yes," she said, "it *was* the Passionate St. John. Daddy bought it last week, and I can play one of the hymn tunes." She played one of the chorale melodies from the St. John Passion.

Then she asked, "Do you know the Grieg Concerto?" I did, and asked if she knew it. She replied, "Gieseking plays it, and I can play the first tune." She played the melody while I played the chords. While it did not sound like Gieseking, it sounded quite a little like Grieg.

As she left the studio, she said, "Daddy plays records every evening. Perhaps I can learn the Chopin Funeral March for my next lesson. Horowitz plays that one."

The following week she played the melody of the first ten measures of the Funeral March. She played it in the original key, B-flat minor. The tune was recognizable, though her fingering was awkward. So I asked her to sing the melody while she clapped the time-values: quarters, dotted-eighths, and sixteenths. Then, keeping a steady rhythm, she played the tune, singing while she did so the numbers of the fingers she was now using:

      Two, Two, two-*Two*-oo

      Two, Two, two-*Two*-oo

      Two, Two, two-*Two, Four,* three-*Three,* two-*Two,* two-*Two*-oo

(The words that are italicized indicate the fingers that come on the beats.)

She found that the fingering of the fifth phrase was easy if she began with her fifth finger on B♭, and used all her fingers in succession:

      Five, four-*Three,* two-*Two, One.*

The phrase is repeated.

Then the third phrase comes once more, with the original fingering.

After she could play the tune smoothly, I showed her the two left-hand chords F B♭ D♭ and G♭ B♭ D♭. She added these chords as a steady accompaniment to the melody.

Eleanor has a small brother, Charlie, who is also musical. So I suggested that she might teach him to play a lower part to the Funeral March. I showed her how he could play alternately B♭ and D♭, over and over in the lower part of the piano, using only the second finger of each hand.

Eleanor reported later that it was lots of fun, and that they played it all the time. She said that she and Charlie tried to play it with Horowitz, but that it was pretty hard and did not go very well.

This bit of ensemble playing came about only because Eleanor's father was interested in talking to his children about music, and in playing records for the family to hear.

Records for Little Children

The younger members of the family will have much pleasure in listening to records. Hundreds have been made of the songs that little children know.

In selecting vocal records for children, it is better to choose those that are sung by a soprano, in the register in which the child himself sings, rather than those sung by a man. On the other hand, a man's *speaking* voice is entirely appropriate in telling stories to children, as in one excellent recording of "Peter and the Wolf."

RECORDING PUPILS' PLAYING

One more aspect of phonograph recordings should be mentioned. That is the recording of the children's own playing. Some teachers have their pupils make records several times a year. The pupils learn a great deal from hearing their own playing, and are often pleasantly, or unpleasantly, surprised. These records also make delightful Christmas presents. Many parents keep them over the years, because they give a running account of their children's progress along the road of piano playing. Hearing these records in succession is like looking over the family photograph album, with pictures of Dennis at the age of 7 in his sailor suit, Dennis at 8 going to dancing school, and Dennis at 9 making a swan dive at an Adirondack camp!

CONCERTS FOR CHILDREN AND YOUNG PEOPLE

In most cities and in many towns, series of concerts are given with programs specially arranged for children of various ages. Walter Damrosch was a pioneer in the movement years ago, and countless children who are now parents themselves owe to him their introduction to music. Never was there a more gifted and beguiling musical personality than his in this field.

Some children might enjoy going to adult concerts occasionally. However, it is often advisable for them to stay for only part of the program (just as many parents take their children to church on Sunday morning, but let them "go home before the sermon.") This is a kindly provision against tiredness and consequent boredom.

If children are taken to an opera, it will certainly add to their enjoyment if they know something of the music and the story beforehand. The Metropolitan Opera Company in New York has special opera performances for young people, and other cities are also attracting young audiences to hear the famous operas.

Choose with care the first opera that your child is to hear. Perhaps because it was my own first experience of an opera, "Lohengrin" seems to me to be an excellent beginning. The story has all the glamor of a fairy tale. I thought it was deeply moving and very beautiful. And I remember as though it were yesterday, longing to go behind the scenes after the second act, to beg Elsa not to ask Lohengrin his name, because it would get her into dreadful trouble! Years later I was speaking to Professor Roy Dickinson Welch's daughter Anne, who was then only ten years old. She had just seen the opera — her first — in Germany. I told her of my experience, and she said, "I felt just that way, too!"

PRACTICING

Practicing is probably the greatest stumbling block in the path of the young piano student, and it is here that the parent can be of greatest help.

Two practical suggestions are that the parent see that the piano is kept in perfect tune, and that the piano keys as well as the young player's hands are clean before they come in contact with each other.

How Much

The amount of time that a child is to practice should be discussed by the parent, the teacher, and the child together. All three should agree on the minimum of time the pupil should spend at the piano in order to get anything done.

It may be difficult for the child to do the same amount of practicing every day, because dancing lessons, Scout meetings, and so many other activities can fill up his afternoons. And on some days, homework for school is heavier than on others.

But he should make a "contract" with himself to do each *week* the amount of time that has been agreed upon. Any practicing done beyond this is plus.

But if the piano lessons are once a week, some practicing should be done every day. He cannot prepare a satisfactory lesson for Monday by doing nothing during the week, and then practicing feverishly on Saturday and Sunday.

Keeping a practice record of the amount of time that they have spent at the piano appeals to some children. But if the child is not interested in keeping such a record, do not force it.

One of my pupils took an impish delight in writing down that he had practiced:

Monday, January 3rd

Chords	3¾ minutes
Czerny Study	9¼ minutes
Mozart Sonata, first page	22½ minutes
Review "Curious Story"	2½ minutes
Sight Reading	7 minutes
TOTAL	**45 minutes**

I asked him if he had also kept a record of the time-out for going over to the clock and making his calculations!

The emphasis in all the foregoing has been on practicing "by the hour." However, some children work much better by the job than "by the hour." All the work in the world is done in one of these two ways. The artist works by the job, the artisan by the hour.

This reminds me of a cartoon in the "New Yorker" magazine a few years ago. It showed a little boy seated in front of a piano. On the bench beside him were a catcher's mitt and a baseball bat, and a ball bulged from one of his pockets. There was a clock on the wall. Peering through the window, and jeering at him, was a group of little boys. His mother was standing by the piano, and the child, looking up hopefully, is saying, "Mom, would you rather have me work hard 20 minutes, or dawdle for an hour?"

What we want every child to realize, of course, is that it is always more a question of the *quality* of work done, than the *quantity*.

I have found with most children that practicing is not in itself the difficulty. Rather it is getting the child to stop what he is doing and start practicing. Once he is at the piano, if he is at all musical, the music itself will take over. Often I have noticed that a child who protests against sitting down and practicing for 15 minutes will, when he has begun to play, go on playing for an hour.

When

The parent and child should work together in deciding when the child shall practice. The most satisfactory results are achieved if some practicing is done at the same time every day. With many children, a short period — even 15 or 20 minutes — before breakfast, or before going to school, insures that something is accomplished at a regular time. Then the rest of the practicing can be done later in the day.

Where

Parents should see that the room in which the child practices is quiet. Studying music takes great concentration, and the child must be constantly listening to what he plays. I have known homes where the piano was in a room through which other children were constantly passing. In one home a child was supposed to practice when, through an open doorway, the other children of the family were watching the program "Disneyland" on television.

If the piano is in the family living room, the parents should see to it that practicing is not done when the room is being used for social purposes. This remark may seem so obvious as to be unnecessary. But I have a memory of one occasion when so-called practicing was being done under impossible conditions. Dinner was over and a little girl was seated at the piano, practicing. At one corner of the room her father and brother were playing checkers. Her mother sat on the divan conversing with a friend. When I came in the mother said that Sarah was going over her music lesson for the following day. I remarked that I did not believe the music lesson was being helped, and she called out to the child, "Do we disturb you, dearie?" Dearie replied in the negative, but continued plodding along while she "went over the lesson." I wondered how the pieces would fare the next day. It made me quite sad, for it seemed such a waste of time, and energy, and money, as well as being such discourtesy to music.

Supervision

The value of parental supervision of the child's practicing is a matter that must be decided by the teacher. It is *not* helpful if a mother who has been brought up on an old-fashioned "method" tries to have the child play her way, when the teacher may be teaching the child something quite different. For example, Mother may have been brought up to count "One-and, Two-and," and the teacher may be using French time-names or English time-values, or the rhythmic counting of beats. If Mother tries to help by insisting on *her* way the child will be hopelessly confused. In any case, the matter of help at home should be discussed by parent and teacher together.

The case is different, obviously, with very little children. Here, help from the parent is usually necessary. Little children will probably not remember what, if anything, they are supposed to practice.

Reports and Rewards

Parents are always interested to receive written reports of their children's progress in their school work, and would probably be interested to have a written report on the music work also.

If the child goes to a music school, these reports would come at regular intervals as a matter of course. If the child is taking lessons from a "private" teacher, a written record of accomplishment is often clarifying for both teacher and parent.

This brings up the whole question of marks for lessons. Some children work well if marks are given, and some do not. It would be deplorable if music were studied with a possible A or B looming up as the important recognition of work done. It is still more deplorable if parental rewards are given or denied in connection with the child's music study. Ideally, a child studies music because he likes it, and not because he can go to the circus if he practices his lesson.

Should Parents Attend Lessons and Pupils' Recitals?

Sometimes a little child does much better with Mother in the room during the lesson, and sometimes quite the reverse. In any event, this, too, is a matter for the teacher to decide. A piano lesson is a time of musical exploration and adventure. Very frequently it is best conducted as a duet rather than a trio.

However, if children are playing in a concert at which an audience is expected, it seems to me very important that as many parents as possible attend.

I remember conducting one School concert where a girl of fourteen, who was a rather nervous child, played fairly well. None of her family was in the audience. Afterwards I met the mother, and said I was sorry she did not hear Constance play. With a shudder she replied, "Oh, I couldn't bear to come and hear her break down."

We talked the matter over and I reported that Constance had not broken down, but that I thought her mother's nervousness about the situation might be communicating itself to the child.

The mother apparently felt that playing in a recital was a sort of unpleasant public examination. Nothing could have been more wide of the mark, as she discovered later. She found that pupils' recitals can be informal and delightful. Eventually she realized that music, instead of causing nervous tension, can be a potent factor in its release.

Parents are usually cooperative with the teacher's aims, if these aims are talked over and understood. I am strongly in favor of meetings of parents and teachers in a group, when matters of general interest can be discussed. Even more important, however, are informal talks between teacher and parent to discuss any problems that have arisen concerning a particular child.

This Part has discussed some of the ways in which all parents can participate in their children's musical development. The degree to which they will do this depends, of course, on the parents' own interest in music, as well as on their feelings of parental responsibility.

The most important thing is for parents to give constant and whole-hearted and intelligent encouragement to their children, as they explore the wonderful world of music.

Part VI. Two Special Cases

THE ADULT BEGINNER

Nowadays more and more older people find themselves with time on their hands which they wish they could use in learning something new and interesting. I would like to suggest that piano playing and the creative study of music make a most stimulating hobby for older people. I do not mean just learning to play pieces, though this is part of the program, but learning how music is made, and adventuring on the piano, exploring chords, and learning what to listen for when great music is played.

Teaching an Adult Beginner is a rewarding experience for the teacher. The adult student is studying music presumably because he wants to, whereas many children take lessons only because of parental pressure.

Many of the adults who come to us for lessons have had some music instruction when they were children, but disliked it so much that as soon as the parental pressure was removed, they no longer played the piano. Now, as adults, they frequently say reproachfully to their parents: "Why did you let me give up taking music lessons?" The parent usually replies, "It was too much work to get you to practice!"

Probably the reason why they hated practicing was that what they had to practice was so uninteresting that they could hardly be enthusiastic about it. Nowadays, fortunately, the musical diet for the beginner, young or old, is far more stimulating and varied than formerly.

A man of forty once came to me for lessons. When I asked him what he wanted to learn, he replied: "I would like to be able to pick out tunes on the piano like 'Fair Harvard' and 'For He's a Jolly Good Fellow.' I would like to play for my little girls to dance. And it would be fun to be able to follow the scores of the operas they broadcast every Saturday. But I can't do any of these things."

I asked if he had ever studied music. He replied that he had "taken piano" for two years, from the time he was nine years old. He had practiced scales and exercises, and had memorized three pieces that his mother made him play whenever there was company. I asked if he still remembered those pieces, and he said, "I was so sick of them that when I stopped taking lessons, I tried hard to forget them!"

This man, in spite of his two years on the piano stool, was, to all intents and purposes, a beginner. And he is probably typical of many of the adults who come to us for lessons.

Like this man, any Adult Beginner has undoubtedly heard much music during his life. He has probably attended concerts; perhaps he has listened to symphony broadcasts over the radio; and he may have a collection of records. The memory of all the music he has ever heard is stored deep in his subconscious mind. This reservoir of musical impressions is a fund of musical experience on which the teacher may draw. The business of the teacher is to help the student bring his subconscious musical impressions up to the level of his conscious mind, so that he may organize and develop them.

The Adult Beginner naturally wants to learn how to play the piano. But he probably will not be able to acquire a fluent technique, since the development of finger facility must begin at an earlier age. His ability to read music, which demands the complicated coordination of eyes and ears and hands, will probably progress slowly.

In spite of these drawbacks, however, he can derive much satisfaction from his piano playing, as well as from his study of music. I would suggest the following curriculum for the Adult Beginner's music study:

1. Studying Keyboard Harmony and Playing by Ear
2. Learning Pieces by Rote
3. Learning to Read Music
4. Listening to and Analyzing Music

All of these four lines of study should proceed simultaneously.

SUGGESTED SYLLABUS OF STUDY
Studying Keyboard Harmony and Playing by Ear

Most adults like to play chords. They can easily learn to play simple chord progressions which they can use as accompaniments to tunes that they whistle or sing. They can also learn to play melodies by ear, and can "vamp" a swing bass accompaniment. They should be taught in the first lesson the use of the pedal. They can also learn to make up melodies and harmonize them with the chords that they are studying.

Most adults are fascinated to discover, through the study of overtones, that chord structure has a mathematical basis. From the construction of the major and minor triads, and from the pattern of tones and half tones in the major and minor scales, they can proceed logically to an understanding of the harmonic and melodic idioms that are an integral part of most of the music they will play.

This study of Keyboard Harmony should include original chord phrases, using the vocabulary that is being studied, and exercises in transposition and modulation. The teacher should illustrate each point that is studied by playing examples from musical literature where the same material is used.

Years ago I taught a middle-aged man who, at the first lesson, learned quickly the circle of major triads, following the pattern of white and black keys. He discovered that with two exceptions the root and the fifth of all the major triads were either two white keys or two black ones, which fitted comfortably under his fingers. These two exceptions were the chords B♭ D F, and B D♯ F♯, where the root and fifth are on keys of opposite colors, which felt, he said, as though they were on the bias. These he immediately labelled "piebald" chords! He had learned to play the circle of thirteen chords in six minutes.

We had been discussing a recent Paderewski recital that we both had attended. I said, "Colonel, these chords that you have played are called Major Triads. It may encourage you to know that Paderewski knows no more major triads than you do, because there are no more!"

His startled exclamation at this point was, "My God!"

Learning Pieces by Rote

There is much music of real value that the Adult Beginner can learn to play by rote, that is, directly on the keyboard, though for some time he could not possibly read these pieces from the printed page. I would teach him such music, for instance, as the Chopin C minor Prelude, Op. 28, and simple arrangements of themes from standard symphonies and operas with which he may already be familiar.

The Bach C major Prelude from the First Book of the "Well-Tempered Clavier," for example, can be taught easily by rote although, of course, not all at one lesson. It should be learned first by playing a solid chord in each measure, instead of the broken chords of Bach's original. The student should follow the finger moves from one chord to the next, and should identify whatever chords he knows. He can learn the piece by rote, a phrase at a time, and the teacher should call his attention to the varying lengths of the phrases. (The piece begins with a four-measure phrase, then two phrases of two measures, then a three-measure phrase, etc.) Working in this way his ear will always be aware of the musical sense of what he is playing.

Also by rote I would teach the Adult Beginner some pieces of lesser musical interest, but of technical value. Through these he can acquire a degree of pianistic freedom, and have the fun of playing all over the keyboard. Pieces that contain much repetition, and with patterns repeated in different octaves of the keyboard, are admirable in giving him a "sense of mastery" of the piano.

A piece learned this way brought spectacular satisfaction to an Adult Beginner whom I once taught. He was a business man, and was going to Europe to join his wife and two children. They were to meet in Switzerland, and he wanted to learn a showy piece that he could play to astonish his loved ones.

His children had both taken piano lessons, but his own piano experience had been limited to picking out a few hymn-tunes by ear. He looked forward to the moment when, in a hotel parlor, he could casually sit down at the piano and launch into a fluent performance of a showy piece. He could not read music, but his ear was excellent and his hands were fairly agile.

We discussed various pieces that I might teach him by rote, and settled on "Sur la Glace à Sweet Briar." (This deservedly popular little piece is cleverly constructed, and can easily be taught by rote. The chord successions sound very grand indeed, but can be learned quite painlessly, simply by following the patterns of finger moves.) This business executive learned to play the piece, pedal and all, in four lessons prior to sailing.

On his return from the European trip I asked how he had succeeded with "Sur la Glace." He reported that the family was stunned. He said that after his first performance, the expressions on their faces reminded him of the picture in a recent advertisement of a French language course. A group of men are seated around a dining room table. One rather smug-looking man is addressing the waiter. Looks of astonishment are on the faces of the rest of the diners, and the caption is "We didn't know that Bill could speak French!"

He also reported that his first question on entering hotels was not "Monsieur, avez-vous deux chambres libres?" but "Monsieur, avez-vous un piano?"

I asked him what he did if people wanted him to play something else. He replied, "Oh, they did that quite often! But I just said, 'Oh, no, I think not. I don't feel in the mood!'"

"Sur la Glace" was performed at every stop during a month's motor trip through Switzerland and France!

Learning to Read Music

I would explain to the Adult Beginner that he will progress quickly in his reading if he will be content to read a great many short and simple pieces, written in a variety of keys and meters. I would give him a beginner's book, preferably a collection of folk tunes that are carefully arranged and edited.

At the first lesson I would acquaint him in a general way with the content of the entire book. The beginning pages will probably be very simple, but he should progress quickly to more interesting pieces. Before he begins to play he should look over the piece as a whole. He should discover what, if any, parts are repeated, also what parts are similar and what are different.

In playing he should train himself to keep his eyes on the notes to avoid "losing his place," and he should play as much as possible by the "touch" system. To help him to keep his eyes following the music and not looking down at his hands, and to keep his mind concentrated on what he is doing, it is a good idea for him to recite aloud, while he plays, some aspect of the printed music: the time values, letter-names of the notes, fingering, and the count.

There are several advantages in using these various reading aids for the beginner, young or old, who is learning to read music. One is that he is always looking at the notes and not at his hands. Another is that he can check that he understands everything on the printed page. In addition, he is probably not getting bored, as might be the case if, while he played, he had done nothing but count "One-Two-Three" over and over. But perhaps the most important is that he really will be teaching himself.

Listening to and Analyzing Music

This is perhaps the most stimulating part of the Adult Beginner's program, because it is broadening his musical horizon far beyond the limits of his own performance. The end of the lesson can be spent in the discussion of a song that he learns by ear, or you may play a recording of an orchestral work, or he may listen to a piano piece that you play for him. You can talk about the music, and call his attention to any interesting points in its structure or development.

This sort of analysis can be more stimulating if several students take part. Even two Adult Beginners discussing music together brings an added element of enthusiasm to the situation. Supposing Mr. A and Miss B, both Adult Beginners, have each planned for a ¾ hour lesson a week. If you can arrange that these two lessons come consecutively and plan your teaching schedule, for example, as follows, it will be greatly to the advantage of each student:

> Mr. A: 3 to 3:30
> Mr. A and Miss B together: 3:30 to 4
> Miss B: 4 to 4:30

The half hour that Mr. A and Miss B are working together could be devoted to a program such as the following: 1) Singing and analyzing by ear a familiar song, such as "Drink to Me Only With Thine Eyes"; 2) a discussion of counterpoint and the structure of a fugue, illustrated by the teacher's playing, for instance, the C minor Fugue from Book 1 of "The Well-Tempered Clavier."

At another lesson the program could be: 1) Singing by ear the St. Anthony Chorale (you may point out the sequential repetitions, and the interesting structure of the piece, with its contrast of five- and four-measure phrase lengths); 2) Playing the record, and discussing the Brahms-Haydn Variations, based on this tune.

At the following lesson the students will probably be interested in seeing the score of the music that is being played. They can follow the notes on the printed page, and can "keep their places" by touching each barline with the right forefinger. This should be done rhythmically, in time with the music. Doing this will be of great help to an Adult Beginner, since this triple sensory correlation of the eyes, the ears, and the fingers is the basis of all sight reading. Following the score in this way will give an over-all sense of the music, and may be called "Reading in the Large."

The four-fold program outlined above will give the Adult Beginner a broad and correlated approach to music, and he will learn much more than if he spends all of his time practicing one long and difficult piece.

By following the suggested syllabus, he will learn something of Keyboard Harmony; he will learn to play by ear; he will learn to play a few adult pieces by rote as well as a few "fancy" ones; he will be able to read many simple pieces; and he will have heard and analyzed some of the world's great music.

This is a varied, rewarding, and nourishing musical diet.

"MAKING OVER" A PUPIL

"Making Over" a pupil is a rather dreadful phrase. But it describes, in the vernacular, a situation that probably every piano teacher has experienced at one time or another.

Students often come to us who have "taken" from another teacher. They may be well developed pianistically, but perhaps are lacking in the understanding of the music that they play. Or, contrariwise, their musical development may be in advance of their pianistic ability.

THE FIRST INTERVIEW

The prospective pupil sits down to play for you. You must use wisdom and sympathy in "sizing up" his performance. He may be very nervous, and you will make due allowance for this.

After he has played, and you have evaluated him in your own mind, begin by telling him what is *good* in his performance. There will surely be something on which you can comment favorably: perhaps the way a certain passage sounded, perhaps his rhythm, perhaps his love of music, perhaps only his industry. After that, tell him what you think is lacking in his musical equipment.

For example, if a student plays all of the notes of the Chopin "Minute Waltz" *in* a minute but, as he dashes along, fails to project much of the meaning of the music, tell him what an asset he has in his fleet fingers — but that now he must come to a better understanding of the musical content of the composition as it unfolds itself under his fingers.

Take time, if possible, to do some musical educating at this first interview. Go over the piece with him in detail, helping him to hear more in the composition than he thought was there. Have him notice, among other things, the charming variety of the phrase lengths, and the exciting little rising sequence leading to the cascade of the descending scale.

You will not play the piece for him and have him merely imitate you. Rather, you will help him to discover for himself more fully the meaning of the composition. If you can do this, "Illumination" will have taken place. As one student said, after he had made what to him were marvelous discoveries, "So, *that's* what it means!" Of course, the piece meant much more than *that,* but he had surely taken a step forward on the path of musical understanding.

167

"Beginning All Over Again"

Do not let your "make-over" pupil think that his time with his previous teacher has been wasted, and that he has to "begin all over again."

I speak feelingly on this point since, as a young student in quest of more technique, I changed teachers on one occasion. The new teacher gave me to understand that I had *no* technique, and that, from her standpoint, I had been taught so badly that I would have to go back to the beginning.

She told me that, in order to acquire a sound technique, I would have to stop playing pieces for at least three months, and practice nothing but technical exercises. She intimated that the method she taught was the only possible way by which I could learn to play the piano. In concluding her diagnosis, she handed me a grudging crumb of comfort, by saying that I was musical. She added that she would be glad to teach me.

I was crushed. I felt that music had died, and that all that was left was the dreary prospect of exercising my hands and fingers in order to play faster and louder.

I stood it for two months, while my knuckles rose and my spirits fell. Then I could "take" it no longer, and stopped the lessons. As I left I was painfully convinced of the truth of the slogan she had reiterated, "The *arch* is the strongest piece of mechanics!"

Really, there is no such thing as "beginning all over again," as though you had never started. No matter what the student has or has not learned, surely, in his previous study, he has acquired *some* knowledge of music that should be recognized and utilized during the rebuilding process.

"Making Over" a Student's Technique

Sometimes you may believe that a student's technique must really be "made over." He may have stiff arms that must be loosened up, or he may have soft, wobbly fingers that must be strengthened and brought under control.

In any event, you must proceed with full sympathetic understanding that you are not working with a machine that is out of order, but with a human being who is seeking your help.

During the process of technical reconstruction, be sure to keep the student's interest in music alive. "Man does not live by bread alone."

And the piano student does not live by acquiring technical proficiency alone. As soon as possible find some piece he may study, which will use the new technique that you are teaching him.

The only object of technical training is to make music sound beautiful, and the sooner technique is put to work in the service of music, the better. For instance, learning to play scales fluently is not an end in itself, but it is a necessary preparation for playing the scales that will be met, for example, in Mozart and Chopin.

The student may be helped to keep musically alert by studying some other aspect of music with which he is not familiar, such as keyboard harmony, or perhaps the beginnings of score reading — anything to keep him aware that the technical exercises that he is practicing are only part of his equipment as a musician.

FINDING HIS MUSICAL LEVEL

The "make-over" pupil may have been playing music that you consider too difficult for him, or too easy, or perhaps rather cheap. In each case, you will want him to acquiesce with a new point of view.

If he comes to you playing music that is far beyond him, you have the delicate task of gently easing him down to the level of music that he can really understand and play well. The pupil who, perhaps, has been taught only long, hard pieces that he cannot interpret or perform adequately should be given a wider musical experience. This can best be accomplished if he learns many short pieces in differing styles, that demand careful study, attentive hearing, and varied technique. At this stage, a student learns more from studying six 1-page pieces than he would from one 6-page piece.

Here you have to be careful to keep up his courage. If his idea of accomplishment has been to play a long piece "without a mistake," he might be discouraged at having to learn simpler, shorter pieces that he may feel are beneath his dignity. But if *you* are eager and excited about the interest and beauty of these smaller pieces, he will catch your excitement.

On the other hand, if you feel sure that a student can play music that is more difficult than that which he brings to you, you have the pleasure of communicating to him this encouraging news. He may have been studying only juvenile literature, and may be quite ready for something more adult.

Perhaps a student's musical experience has been confined to pieces that, although showy and brilliant, you feel are musically rather trivial and tawdry. You will use judgment in introducing him to a better class of literature. This you will have to do gradually. You can hardly expect him immediately to transfer his interest from his facile performance of "The Rippling Waters of Minnehaha" to the serious study of a Bach Prelude and Fugue.

REVAMPING HIS OLD REPERTORY

After he has learned, through the compositions that he is now studying, to have a wider perspective on the meaning of *all* music, it is a good idea to go over some of his "old pieces" with him. He will discover how much more he *now* hears in a piece that he thought he knew quite well when he first studied it.

The "make-over" pupil often says, "If I had only known this five years ago," or "twenty-five" — as the case may be. It is well to assure him that things happen to us in life as soon as we are ready for them, and that *now* is the "appointed time." Assure him that on the road he is now traveling, wider and wider vistas of musical experience will continually open before him.

Help him to realize that there is no end to what can be discovered about a great composition. Studying music is a continuing process of unfoldment. During his study of a composition it will reveal itself more and more.

No actor could feel that he had given the final, perfect performance of "Hamlet." As, during the years, he himself grows mentally and spiritually, so also will grow his conception of the "melancholy Dane."

When Toscanini planned to record the Ninth Symphony of Beethoven, which during his long life he had conducted many times, he spent hours in studying the score anew, before beginning rehearsals.

In conclusion, let us remember that as teachers our first responsibility to a student is to help him continuously to make *himself* over. We wish him to make his own discoveries and to come to his own decisions. We want only that he may be an independent traveler, as he journeys in the realm of music.

Part VII. "Listening In"

The following section of this book consists of reports of various lessons and interviews with students of all ages. Many of them were pupils of my own. Some, however, were pupils of other teachers who had asked if I would hear their students play. In these cases, the pupils, accompanied by their teachers, came for a single interview, which started as an audition, but usually ended up as a lesson, in which I tried to help the student hear and understand more of the content of what he was playing.

Many lessons were recorded at the time. They are given here, not, in any sense, as examples of how lessons *should* be given, but as "documentary evidence" of how some lessons *were* given to students of varying degrees of musical aptitude and accomplishment.

MONA

"Hot Cross Buns" — The Scale of C

Mona, a bright little six-year-old, came in one day while I was playing. She stood beside the piano, listening, and then said: "Could I play on your piano? We haven't any at home." I replied, "Of course, but first, won't you sing a song for me?"

Her voice was true and her rhythm good, and she sang "Jingle Bells" while I played an accompaniment. (Most children seem to be born knowing "Jingle Bells"! One wonders, in this day of automobiles and planes, what their idea of a "one-horse open sleigh" can be!)

Mona said, *"Now,* can I play a piece?"

We began by singing and clapping the tune of "Hot Cross Buns" together.

Hot cross buns! Hot cross buns! One a pen-ny, Two a pen-ny, Hot cross buns!

171

I showed her how to play it with her right forefinger. (Wasn't it Robert Louis Stevenson who said he investigated the piano with a "melodious forefinger"?)

I did not teach her the letter names of the keys, but I started her on E, and showed her how to play "Hot Cross Buns" on the three white keys E D C. I played chords to harmonize the melody. Next she played the tune beginning on A, playing A G F, and then beginning on B, playing B A G — both of which turned out successfully. I suggested that she try three black keys, and started her on Bb, and she played the tune, using the keys Bb Ab Gb. These turned out all right, because the notes were a whole step apart, and she played either three white keys or three black ones. I supplied a harmonization in all these keys.

Next I put her finger on G, and asked her to try beginning there, and said that something strange was going to happen. She played G F E, and discovered at once that E "sounded horrid," which indeed it did, as I was playing the Eb major triad. She quickly found that she would have to play a black key, Eb, instead of the white key E.

I wanted her to be able to transpose "Hot Cross Buns" into any key, and know what she was doing, so I began by showing her how to play the chromatic scale down. I put her right forefinger on C, and asked her to go on down the piano, playing every white or black key she came to, and singing the color names, white or black, as she touched each key. She did this, singing, "White, White, Black, White, Black, White, etc." until she reached the C below.

We then went back to "Hot Cross Buns." I told her that this time she could begin on any black or white key that she wished, and she chose to begin on G#. I asked her to play that key, then to skip the next key (G), to play the next one (F#), to skip the next one (F), and to play the next one (E). She did this, playing G#, F#, E, and saying aloud, "Play, Skip, Play, Skip, Play."

Using this pattern, she was soon playing "Hot Cross Buns" all over the piano. At one point I tried to help her as I thought she was about to make a mistake, but she swept my hand off the keyboard, and said, "Let me do it all by myself!" I realized that Mona was reminding me of one of my own teaching precepts, "Don't *teach* children, let them learn!"

Mona was learning so quickly that I said, "Wouldn't it be fun if we made up a piece together?" I asked her how far she could count, and she answered, "Way past a hundred!" I told her that in music she only had to go as far as eight.

I put her right forefinger on middle C, and asked her to walk this finger up the piano on white keys, counting from 1 to 8. Walking up the keys this way was like climbing up a ladder. The name of a musical ladder is a Scale.

Next I asked her if she could play and sing slowly just the keys 1 and 3 and 5. Then she played and sang both the scale and the broken chord coming down.

This is the tune and the accompaniment that we made up together:

In technical language, Mona had learned:

1. To transpose "Hot Cross Buns" into any key, playing a pattern of whole steps.
2. To play the chromatic scale downwards.
3. To sing and play the scale and broken chord of C major, ascending and descending.

This completed her first adventure in piano playing. I later learned that on her return home she had demanded a piano for Christmas!

SKIPPY

"Raindrops" — Triads — The Dominant Seventh Chord

Skippy is a seven-year-old who was just beginning his second year of piano lessons. His teacher, who had been a student of my own, asked if I would hear him play. He came with his mother and his teacher. He was a shy little boy. For the first minutes of our interview, he kept glancing apprehensively across the room to where his mother was seated, as though measuring the distance between them, so that he could run to cover in case of need! But, as he realized that I was as much interested in the music he was making as I was in him as a person, things quieted down, and he began to have a good time.

First he played quite nicely a little piece called "Raindrops." The fingers playing the melody moved easily and quickly, but the accompanying chords were a bit heavy. I asked him if he had ever noticed how lightly raindrops bounce when they hit the sidewalk, or how the last few drops of water sometimes bounce in the bathtub, when you turn off the faucet. I suggested that in playing the chords his whole arm way up to his shoulder must be light, or the raindrops would sound clumsy.

He caught the idea at once. He played the piece again, with a featherweight accompaniment, and this time his raindrops were entirely satisfactory.

His teacher remarked that Skippy liked chords. I said that I loved chords, and asked him which ones he knew. He replied: "I can play all the triads in lots of major scales, and tell you their names, and I know some dominant seventh chords."

I said, "Do play the triads in C major, and I wonder if you could sing the root letters as you go along."

He did so, playing the chords, and singing: "C major, D minor, E minor, F major, G major, A minor, B diminished, and C major."

His voice was true, and I realized that he had an excellent ear.

I asked him to play the first four triads again, and to say only what *kind* they were. He played the chords on C, D, E, and F, saying as he played, "Major, minor, minor, Major."

A.D.:   Skippy, do you see that these four chords make a sort of
          pattern?

174

Skippy: Let's see. Do you mean that there are majors on the outside, and minors in the middle?

A.D.:   Yes, that's just what I *do* mean. Now play the last four chords, and see if there's any pattern there.

He played the chords of the second half of the scale, on G, A, B, and C. He discovered that these made a slightly different pattern, and said, "The outside ones are major, but one of the inside ones is minor, and the other is diminished. Does it work that way in all the scales?"

A.D.:   Why don't you try it in another scale and see?

He played the triads in F major, and was pleased to discover that the pattern "worked."

A.D.:   Skippy, here's something else about chords. Do you know that they "push" tones around? Sometimes they push tones up, and sometimes they push tones down. Like this!

I gave him a gentle shove to the right, and said, "You see, you're being pushed *up* the piano!" Then I shoved him to the left and said, "Now you're being pushed *down* toward the bass. Let's play a game, where different chords push the same tone around to different places. *You* can play the tone, and *I* will play the chords. Of course, I'm not really going to push *you* around any more, but you'll have to hear where my chords are going to push your tone. We could call the game, 'Which Way and How Far'."

Skippy: Which note shall I play?

A.D.:   You can play the G above middle C, and I will make it go to four different places. You'll have to listen very carefully. Then you play the key that comes next, and I'll play the chord that comes next. Of course, your G will sound different every time. That's another thing that chords do — they make melody tones sound different, and can really change their meaning.

           Now, you're the tone, and I'm the accompaniment. Let's begin.

He played G, and beneath it I played E♭-B♭-D♭ (the dominant seventh of A-flat, of which his G was the leading tone). I said, "Listen to where my chord is pushing your G. Are you going up or down?" and he said, "I'm going up." He played A♭, while I resolved the chord to A-flat major.

Again he played his G, and below it I played C-E-B♭. He heard that he was traveling down, and moved his G to F, while I resolved this dominant seventh to F major.

Next I played A-C♯-E beneath his G. He moved to F♯, while I

played D major. He said, "I could have gone to F." He repeated his G, and then as he moved it to F, I played the D minor triad, and said, "You certainly could!"

Skippy: They both sound right!

A.D.:   The next one's going to be harder. I think you'll find that you have to make two moves to really end the tune. You'll have to listen very carefully.

While he played his G again, I played F-A-C-E♭ (which made his note the top of a dominant ninth chord). He seemed surprised, and said, "Next I can play F," and he did so, while I still held my chord.

Skippy: But the tune isn't finished!

He was now, of course, on a dominant seventh chord. I hoped he would hear the resolution of F to B♭.

A.D.:   I think here you'll have to do some jumping.

Skippy: Would B♭ do?

A.D.:   That would be fine!

So he played B♭, and I played the B♭ triad adding a B♭ octave in the bass to make a final ending.

These are the chord progressions that we played:

A.D.:   There are lots of other places I could have "pushed" you, but that's enough for today.

Skippy turned to his teacher and volunteered: "Those were all dominant sevenths that she played!"

And his teacher beamed!

So many teachers teach piano playing exclusively that it was a pleasure to find that Skippy's ears and mind were being trained as well as his fingers.

I wish that all piano teachers would recognize that ear training is the basis of all music study.

DAVID

"THE WILD HORSEMAN" — "THE HAPPY FARMER" — PHRASING
— HEARING THE DOTS — "MUSICAL QUESTIONS AND ANSWERS"

David was a gifted eight-year-old. His teacher, who brought him
to play for me, told me that he was very pianistic, that he had perfect
pitch, and that he read music so well that when she gave him a new
piece to learn he came back having read most of the pieces in the book.
She said he always played so fast that it was difficult to hold him back,
and added that he was at the piano all the time.

This last was apparent immediately, for while she and I were talking, David had seated himself at the piano, and was playing chords up
and down and little bits of a dozen pieces. He seemed unable to keep
his fingers away from the keyboard. He acted, I thought, like a thirsty
little puppy, eagerly lapping up water that he had just discovered.

I sat down beside him and said, "You like music a lot, don't you,
David?" "Yes, I do," he replied. "And now I'll play 'The Wild Horseman' and 'The Happy Farmer'."

He played these two pieces with great gusto and fluency. Both went
along at a terrific speed. When he had finished, I commented, "David,
I think you have chosen two of the hardest pieces in the book. You
certainly play them as though you enjoy them. And a great deal of
what you do is good. But there are some details in each piece that you
didn't hear, because you played so fast and furiously. Begin 'The Wild
Horseman' again, and play the first four measures slowly."

David played these measures slowly, counting aloud, "Six-*One*-Two-
Three, *Four*-Five-Six, etc." with two heavy triplets in each measure.

"I suppose the phrasing might go that way," I said, "but it doesn't
sound much like a wild horseman, does it? You know, very often, using
words can help to straighten out phrasing. Instead of counting, let's see
if we can find some words that will fit the tune. The way you played it,
the words might be, 'I'm galloping, galloping.' But I think it would
sound better if the words were, 'I gallop, I gallop.' Let me play the
first four measures of the piece both ways, and see if you can hear
the difference."

I did so, and David's quick ear caught the difference between the
two groupings. He said that he liked the second way best, and we

worked out the following words to fit the melody of these four measures:

> I gallop,
> I gallop,
> To Paris I gallop,
> To Paris I gallop,
> To Paris I go.

David wrote these words down in his notebook, at my dictation, putting a comma at the end of each line, thus grouping the words as the notes of the tune are grouped. He discovered that this rhythmic grouping of the melody continues through the piece: it is played six times — twice in the right hand, twice in the left hand, and twice again in the right.

Then David played the piece once more, saying this jingle over and over while he played. His playing had slowed down, and he was now phrasing more musically, and listening to what he was doing. The Wild Horseman galloped along with much greater ease and rhythmic conviction, and the piece sounded far more exciting.

I said, "David, that sounds ever so much better. I hope you think so, too." And he answered, "I've played it so long the other way, it's hard to change. But I guess it does sound better. Still, the music *looks* just like the way I played it at first." "You're quite right," I said. "But you have to read music with your ears as well as your eyes! If this piece were written nowadays, I think the composer would have printed the tune rather differently, so that it would have been easier to read it with the grouping we have worked out."

Now we turned to "The Happy Farmer," and I asked David to play it once more. He raced through the piece *fortissimo,* and, like most little boys, played the right-hand accompanying chords with a vigorous thump-*thump!*

"Well, you and the farmer certainly had a happy time together," I commented. "But you went so fast that I don't think you heard the dots." David was puzzled. "What do you mean — hear the dots?"

I answered, "Well, they are very important, and quite often they are the loudest things in a measure. Let's leave 'The Happy Farmer' for a moment and talk about dots. There are lots of dots, for instance, in 'My Country, 'Tis of Thee.' Can you play the tune by ear? Try it, beginning on G, and sing the words while you play."

David found the notes easily and sang the tune, but the time-values were not entirely steady. I got out a copy of the song, and together we pointed to the notes of the melody, and sang the time-values: "Quarter Quarter Quarter| Quarter Dot-Eighth Quarter| etc." David had done a great deal of counting all his life, but he had never identified time-values in this way, and he found it quite amusing.

Then he played the melody again, still singing the time-values. Every time he came to a dot, I gave him a little push on his knee, so that he could feel the additional lengthening of the tone, and could feel the rhythmic impulse of the "push" of the dot toward the following note. He discovered that in "My Country, 'Tis of Thee" there are seven measures in which dots occur — there are five dotted quarters and two dotted halves in the tune.

When he understood this, I said, "Now let's see about the dots in 'The Happy Farmer'." We got out the music, and I asked, "Will you play the left-hand melody of the first eight measures, and sing the time-values aloud, just as you did in 'My Country, 'Tis of Thee.' And wait on every dot until you're sure you've heard it."

David was most responsive. He played the left-hand part of "The Happy Farmer," singing "Eighth| Quarter-Dot, Eighth-Quarter-Dot, Eighth| Two-Eighths, Two-Eighths, Quarter-Dot, etc."

"You see, the left-hand part has quite a few dots, doesn't it?" I said. "And you heard them all! Now we can add the right-hand chords. They, of course, are just an accompaniment, and you must hold your arm very light while you play them, or else they will be so loud that they will drown out the melody. See if you can play the first eight measures of this piece with both hands together, playing the left-hand melody with a legato touch, and the right-hand chords quietly with a light arm."

David was an unusually pianistic little boy, and he played these eight measures very nicely, hands together, balancing the two touches.

This brought us to the middle section of the piece, measures 9 through 12. These measures are really quite difficult pianistically, because both hands have to play melodic lines and also light chord tones. We studied it this way:

First David played the bass melody of these four measures alone, singing the time-values. Then, still singing the time-values, he played the melodic line in the right-hand part alone, leaving out the chord notes. Next he played these two melodies together, and discovered that the two tunes "matched" exactly in time-values and in direction.

All that was left to do in this passage was to add the accompanying chord tones in each hand. At first, when he tried it, David's thumbs came bumping down, disturbing the melodic lines. But he found that if he tipped his hands slightly toward the little fingers, the weight would be kept off the thumbs, and he could play the chord tones lightly. He was quick at learning these little tricks of pianism.

The next two measures are so like the beginning of the piece that they presented no difficulty. David remembered the different feelings in his two hands: arm-weight in the left-hand melody, and feather-weight in the right-hand accompaniment.

The piece ends with the last six measures repeated, so there was nothing new to learn.

Finally he played the piece straight through. It was a great improvement over his first stormy performance. I thought David had shown great character to be willing to play slowly, and to listen, and to study so carefully a piece that he had probably rattled through one hundred times. I told him, "That sounded ever so much better, David. You know, the first time you played this piece, it was so fast that I couldn't hear anything that was going on. The happy farmer could have been racing to a fire, instead of returning from his work — as you see he was from the title of the piece. By the way, why do you suppose Schumann gave this piece that name?"

David replied: "I don't know. I never thought about it."

I said, "Well, I suppose he had some sort of story in his mind. Let me play it, and talk about what he might have meant."

I played the piece, and my running commentary as I played went something like this:

"Here is Mr. Farmer walking happily along the road, coming home from his work in the fields, and singing cheerfully in the bass. Perhaps the chords are a sort of background scenery he is passing by. Then Mrs. Farmer comes to meet him. First she sings a little song that goes nicely with his. Then she decides to sing part of his song with him. But he finishes the tune alone. They repeat their little duet. But he has the last word to say. At the end, they probably go into the house together and have supper."

When I had finished playing, I said, "Schumann probably didn't have exactly *this* story in his mind when he composed 'The Happy Farmer,' but it could have been something like it, don't you think so?" David's answer was a noncommittal "Maybe"!

We ended the lesson by playing a game on the piano called "Musical Questions and Answers." I made up a four-measure melody, and asked David to play an answering phrase. He had not been encouraged to improvise, so at first he only imitated me, repeating my phrase, perhaps changing one or two notes. But little by little his real musical gift began to show itself, and we improvised a number of quite interesting melodies together. Then we reversed the order, David "making up" the first phrase, and I playing an answering one. He obviously enjoyed this kind of musical game, and I felt that the creative side of his musical talent could certainly be developed.

I thought to myself, "What a piquing and delightful small boy! And what fun it must be to teach him!"

The lesson was over. My last comment was, "You know, David, besides writing music for children, like 'The Happy Farmer' and 'The Wild Horseman,' and the other pieces in the 'Album for the Young,' Schumann also wrote a little book of Advice for Young Musicians. One of the things he said might have been written specially for you. He is talking about people who practice exercises faster and faster, and he says, 'That is about as sensible as trying to pronounce A B C quicker and quicker every day.' The main thing *you* have to guard against, David, is playing too fast! . . . Schumann's last piece of advice was perhaps the wisest of all. He said, 'Study is unending.' That is what we have been doing this last hour — studying 'The Wild Horseman' and 'The Happy Farmer.' There is still more for you to discover in both these pieces. And I hope I'll hear you play them again sometime."

As I turned to say goodbye to his teacher, David was back at the piano, playing "The Happy Farmer" not as he had first played it, *Prestissimo con fuoco,* but now, *Allegro, ma con amore!*

SUSIE

(This lesson is reported verbatim. Susie speaks for herself!)

(Seven-and-a-half-year-old Susie was an engaging and voluble little extrovert. Miss B., her young teacher, who had been a pupil of my own, brought Susie to play for me.

Susie started by playing the "Vesper Song" from the "First Solo Book." Her tone was good, her hand position was excellent, but her rhythm was very unsteady.)

A.D.:   Susie, it sounds as though you were playing two different pieces — a slow one and a fast one. Did you know that you played the second part almost twice as fast as the first part?

Susie (with surprise): I *did?* Sometimes I do that.

A.D.:   Yes, you did, and we will have to fix it. Let's see if you can match the first part and the second part, so that they sound like the same piece, which they really are! First get a good, steady count. What is the count of the first part?

Susie: It's "Two-*One*," and it sounds like churchbells ringing.

A.D.:   Is the count the same all the way through the piece?

Susie: Why, no! On the third line it goes "*One*-Two."

A.D.:   Well, I never would have guessed it from the way you played! The count is different in the second part, but it isn't any faster. Now, Susie, don't play, but sing and count the melody all the way through.

(We did this together. When her counting was steady, I asked her to play the piece again. We both sang and counted while she played, and I gently tapped an alternate shoulder on each beat. This time her rhythm was steady.)

A.D.:   That's much better! You see you *can* do it. Rhythm is inside of you, you know. I tapped your shoulders just to remind you of what the steady beats *feel* like, so that you wouldn't get off the track . . . Do you know what Rhythm means?

Susie: It's whether you go fast or slow.

A.D.:   Yes, and it's also whether you keep going steadily. Rhythm

183

is not something you learn, like scales. It's something that you *feel* inside. You breathe in rhythm, and you talk in rhythm. And before you begin to play a piece on the piano, you should sit quietly for a moment, until you feel inside just how fast the piece wants to go. Then, when you play, you keep it going steadily at that speed.

Susie: It sounded better then, didn't it?

A.D.:   Much better! But you did it after we had been practicing it. Now the point is, can you play it that way the first time? When you're playing a piece, do you want to do it right the first time or the seventeenth time?

Susie: The first time, of course.

A.D.:   Wouldn't it be funny if a man came out on the stage at a concert and started to play, and his piece didn't go quite right, and he turned around to the audience and said, "Excuse me, ladies and gentlemen, I'm going to start that again!"

Susie: Why, if that happened, I'd leave the concert!

A.D.:   And so would I! You see, you should decide beforehand how fast or slow you're going to play a piece, shouldn't you?

Susie: You certainly should!

(Susie had concentrated well so far in the lesson. I wanted to get her mind away from the "Vesper Song" for a few moments, and then have her go back to the piano and see if she could play the piece steadily the first time. So I took her to the window and showed her our birds' feeding station. We then had an animated conversation about what birds like to eat. Susie informed me that she fed her canary peanut butter.)

A.D.:   Now, I've learned something! I never knew that birds liked peanut butter! And *you've* learned something — how easy it is to keep the beats steady in "Vesper Song." So now each of us has an idea we never had before! Here's something I heard the other day — see if you can understand it. "If I give you a dollar, and you give me a dollar, we each have a dollar. But if I give you an idea, and you give me an idea, we each have two ideas!" That's what's happened to us!

Susie: It sounds like arithmetic!

A.D.:   Yes, it does. Now let's see if you remember the idea I gave you. What are you going to do before you play "Vesper Song" again?

Susie: I'm going to think in my head before I start about how fast it goes, and then I'll keep the beat steady.

A.D.:   Susie, you couldn't be more right!

(This time she played the piece through with rhythmic steadiness.)

A.D.: Now I think "Vesper Song" is a lovely piece. But before, the way you played it, I thought it was crazy.

Susie: You did? No, it's a *pretty* piece. It depends on who's playing it — if you play it right or if you play it all crazy.

A.D.: Susie, you certainly know all the answers! I'll tell you a story about this piece.

(I told her about a visit I once had with the famous English pianist Dame Myra Hess. I was showing her the "First Solo Book" and some second piano accompaniments I had just written to go with the pieces. Besides being a great artist, Dame Myra is interested in music education, and I asked her if she would be willing to read a few of the pieces with me. She opened the two grand pianos, and when we came to the "Vesper Song", she played it meticulously, changing the count from "Two-*One*" to "*One*-Two." At the conclusion of our performance, I said, "Dame Myra, I have played this piece with many pianists, and you are the only one on a first reading to hold that half note at the end of the second line for two beats!" She laughed, and said, "Miss Diller, I was counting very carefully all the way through!" Susie got the point.)

Susie: Well, she's a concert pianist — she *should* know!

(I asked Susie if she would like to play something else, and she produced another book and put it on the music rack.)

A.D.: What's the name of the piece you're going to play now?

Susie: I don't know.

A.D.: Goodness, don't you know the names of your friends?

(Susie opened the book and found the place.)

Susie: Oh yes, it's a Sonatina by Clementi in C major. Do you know it?

A.D.: Yes, I do, but it's quite a long time since I've heard it.

Susie: It's a nice piece, too.

(She proceeded to play, until I stopped her at the double bar after the first 15 measures. Her phrasing had been completely unclear.)

A.D.: Susie, do you know what a phrase is in music?

Susie: It's notes that go together.

A.D.: Yes, it's just like words that go together in English, or any other language. If you group the wrong ones together, it doesn't make sense. The way you phrased the Sonatina didn't make much sense.

Susie: But I was counting to myself "*One*-Two-Three-Four" all the time, and those go together, don't they?

A.D.:   Let's try it and see. Let's work on the right hand alone.
           Play the first four measures again, and count aloud "*One-
           Two-Three-Four.*" Make a long hold on every "Four," and
           see if you really do believe that those notes go together.
(She played it, making an elaborate hold on each fourth count.)

Susie: It sounds funny.
A.D.:   Let's see if we can discover what notes Clementi meant to
           go together.
(I looked out the window, trying to think of words that we might sing
to the melody of the first four measures, so that Susie would hear the
rhythm and phrasing correctly.)
A.D.:   These words would fit: "Trees are green.
                                      The trees are green.
                                      The trees in the garden are lovely and green."
Susie: That's pretty!
A.D.:   Thank you. Now try this. Sing those words while you play
           the melody alone.
(Susie did so.)

Susie: They fit very well.

A.D.:   Now you'll find that counting "*One*-Two-Three-Four" *doesn't* fit very well! When you counted that way, it was just as though you said:

           "Trees are green The.

           Trees are green The."

Susie: People don't talk like that! That's silly!

A.D.:   Yes, and counting "*One*-Two-Three-Four" in this piece sounds silly.

Susie: But how would you count it?

A.D.:   I'd count it: "*One*-Two-Three

           Four *One*-Two-Three

           Four *One*-Two-Three Four-*One*-Two-Three-Four."

Play it again, Susie, and count it that way.

(Susie did, and her phrasing was much improved.)

A.D.:   And now Mr. Clementi, wherever he is, is saying "Thank you, Susie, you played just what I meant!"

Susie: I'm glad he liked it!

A.D.:   Susie, play it once more, to be sure you have it right — just the right hand alone.

(This time Susie used a wrong fingering in the descending passage in the third measure. She crossed over to B with the second finger instead of the third, and found herself in the fourth measure one finger short.)

A.D.:   Susie, now you're stuck! I never saw anyone named Susie in a bigger jam than you are at this moment!

Susie: I know, I used the wrong finger.

A.D.:   Susie, what's the point of fingering?

Susie: Because if you don't use the right fingers, you run out of fingers, and then you can't play the piece.

A.D.:   Well, that's just what happened here. Do it once more.

(The ascending scales in measures 8 and 10 were the next problem.)

A.D.:   Take each note upstairs with you, Susie! For goodness sake, look at the music! You see, this is just a scale, isn't it? And it's in the key of G — you know that.

Susie: Yes, you can't know anything about music unless you look at the page.

A.D.:   Well, you looked at the page, but you didn't *see* it. There's a difference, isn't there! It depends on what you see when you look. I wonder if you know there's a sequence there, too. Did you ever meet a sequence?

Susie: Yes, lots of times.

A.D.:   Well, you missed this one! Here is a sequence to see, and
         to hear, and to feel with your fingers. Susie, this is a wonder-
         ful chance for you to learn how to drive a car. What do
         you suppose makes a good driver?

Susie: If you see far ahead and know where you're going, I guess.

A.D.:   Right again! And it's the same way with your playing these
         sequences. You've got to look ahead, and see that you don't
         fall into a ditch or run into a telephone pole. You've got
         to think your music ahead, too, just as you would look ahead
         if you were driving a car.

(Again Susie showed her quickness in grasping exactly what I meant.
She was now phrasing the melody in the right hand beautifully.)

A.D.:   Now, Susie, the great moment has arrived! Let's see if you
         can play as far as we've gone with both hands together.
         Remember, look ahead, and hear ahead!

(With all the good intentions in the world, Susie's old habits asserted
themselves, and the piece played with both hands together fell apart.)

Susie: That was awful.

A.D.:   You think so? But the person who's having the most dreadful
         time of all is Mr. Clementi. Because he's depending on *you,*
         Susie.

Susie: I guess it needs a little more thinking.

A.D.:   A *little* more? How much, 2 cents worth?

Susie: No, a *lot* more; $5.85 cents worth!

A.D.:   Yes, and remember, you do your thinking and your practic-
         ing not *next* week, but *last* week! You don't buy your
         Christmas presents on New Year's Day, do you?

Susie: Of course not! You do it before. And I guess I've got to do
         my thinking before I play the piece, too.

(Now I played the Clementi Sonatina through, as far as we had gone,
so that the last impression of this piece in Susie's ears would be a
musical one. Then, to give variety to her lesson, we played some chords,
and did some ear training together. With about five minutes left of the
lesson, I asked Susie if she had any idea what I was going to ask her
to play before she went home.)

Susie: I know, "Vesper Song."

A.D.:   That's right. Do you know why?

Susie: To see if I remember it all and can play it the first time.
         You know, this is a nice piece. It's like people taking a walk,
         when it's nice and cool, you know — maybe going to church.
         And they're talking all the time . . . it's like . . . like maybe

if you were singing a baby to sleep, you'd be so very soft and quiet.

A.D.:   Do you know a lot about babies?

Susie: Yes, I have a baby sister. I'm seven and a half, but she's only a baby. I'll be glad when I get to be ten — then I'll be a baby-sitter.

(After some discussion of this fascinating profession [and I learned that baby-sitters get a dollar an hour], we got back to the music. Unfortunately Susie's old habits took over, and the piece was again played in two speeds. But she caught herself immediately.)

Susie: Oh, if I play that part so fast, the baby will be giggling all night long!

A.D.:   Yes, and if the baby giggles all night long, because you play that part so fast, you'll be worth only about 5 cents as a baby-sitter! Remember, Susie, don't start to play the piece until you're absolutely sure inside of yourself what you're going to say and tell the baby through your music.

(This time it went perfectly.)

(We had been working for almost an hour, and it was time for Susie to go home.)

A.D.:   It has been nice working with you, Susie, and I think you have learned a lot. What do *you* think you have learned?

Susie: Look out for the rhythm, and use the right fingers, and play it right the first time.

A.D.:   How about Clementi?

Susie: Oh, yes, listen to the phrasing. And then we talked about sequences and look ahead and think ahead — and lots of other things. I liked it all.

A.D.:   Will you play for me again in about a month, and see if all the things we talked about are better?

Susie: I'll try.

(And on this hopeful note she left the room. Miss B. stayed on a few moments, and we discussed Susie's problems. She told me that she felt inadequate in dealing with Susie, and said: "Susie always leads the lesson. Her mind is like quicksilver. She's so fast, instead of being two steps ahead of her, I'm a couple behind her!" I reminded her that we learn to teach only by doing it. Since there was a strong feeling of sympathy between her and Susie, I thought that this unusual child was Miss B.'s Opportunity No. 1 in the teaching field. I told Miss B. that I looked forward to hearing the imaginative little chatterbox soon again.)

FAITH

Chopin A major Prelude, Op. 28, No. 7

Faith is a charming little ten-year-old neighbor, who had studied the piano for two years with a teacher to whom she was devoted. She telephoned me one day, and asked if I would help her with the Chopin A major Prelude which she was trying to learn as a surprise for her teacher.

The piece was so much more difficult than any of the music I knew she had been playing that I asked her if she could play all the notes, and she said, "All of them, except that hard chord. I *cannot* play those notes!"

So I suggested that she come over and that we study the piece together.

This innocent-looking little piece is really more difficult than it appears. The difficulties for an inexperienced player are to realize the rhythmic count, "Three-*One*-Two," with its slight rubato, and also to hear the groupings of the notes in the melody with a sufficient pause on the dotted eighth notes, then letting the sixteenths move swiftly to the following chords, and also not to thump out the reiterated chords.

Hundreds of little girls are eager to play this piece, so it may be of interest to recount how one little girl studied it and was able to play it quite presentably in a short time.

Faith arrived, and played the piece through. The notes were correct, but the rhythm was unsteady.

So the first thing to do was to establish the rhythmic design, the count of the piece, in her ear and in her body. She knew that the count of the piece is "Three-*One*-Two," but she did not feel this. So first she practiced the conductor's gestures, moving her right arm with a continuous motion Up-Down-Out, and counting aloud, "Three-*One*-Two." She repeated the gesture several times, until she felt the swing of the rhythm. Then I played the piece, while she continued conducting. She found that in order to match my playing, the motion in her arm slackened very slightly on the end of the rhythmic design, the count "Two."

Next she worked on playing the melodic line in the right hand, omitting the chords. The melody of this piece is made of eight two-measure phrases, in which the time-values are identical. Sometimes

190

using words that fit a melody is helpful in giving the rhythmic feeling of the melodic line, so I suggested that while she played the melody, she sing the words, "I love to dance and sing," for each of the phrases. This brought the grouping of the tones perfectly: "I love" insured that she held the dotted eighths for their full value; "to dance" insured that the sixteenth notes moved swiftly to the following quarters, and "and sing" grouped the last two tones of each phrase rhythmically. She played the melody all the way through, singing these words while she played. Now the rhythmic design was clear, and the time-values were played accurately.

Faith had been studying intervals, so she was interested to compare the relative size of the intervals in the melody where the sixteenth notes move so quickly to the following tones. She played these "spots" in the melody, saying as she did so: "First you go down a third, D to B; then up a fourth, E to A; then up a third, B to D; then up another third, A to C♯. In the second half of the piece, like the beginning, you go down a third, D to B; then up a sixth, E to C♯; then up a third, D to F♯; and finally up an octave, A to A." She played these intervals in succession, using a slight rotary motion of the upper arm to help connect the tones. She volunteered that playing the intervals this way was like reading a poem, and saying only the words that rhymed at the end of each line.

Now we analyzed the left-hand part, as we had done the right-hand melody. First she played the succession of ten low bass notes, omitting the following chords. She found that the bass notes made a tune, such as the 'cellos might play in an orchestra. They went E to A, E to A, E to A to F♯, B to E to A. She did this slowly, playing the notes with the fifth finger, and clinging to each key, until she was sure that she heard the tone clearly. To establish the relationship of these low bass notes and the melody, she played the bass line once more, while she *sang* the melodic line. Then she played the left-hand part as written, with the chords, and realized that these low bass notes were the harmonic support of the entire piece.

Following this, she played the right-hand melody and left-hand part together, but still omitting the right-hand chords.

After this had been successfully accomplished, she practiced the right hand part alone, adding the chords to the melody. And, finally, she put everything together.

We spent a little time "fixing up" the F♯ chord. She found that she could play it easily if it was slightly simplified, and if she divided the notes between the two hands; left hand, F♯ C♯ F♯: right hand,

A♯ C♯ E A♯; then moving her left arm freely from the shoulder, cross-ing over to the high C♯ with her left hand 3rd finger standing high on C♯, as though it were standing on a mountain top, admiring the view. Her delighted comment was, "I didn't think that I could ever play that hard chord, but now I can gather it all up in both hands!" She realized that this was the climax of the whole piece, and that she must play the F♯ chord deliberately, so that everyone would know that this was the high-spot, and would have time enough to hear it. After this, the music gradually subsides.

The mechanics of the piece were now quite well established, and she was certainly hearing very much more than she had at first. So I said that I would like to hear her play the whole piece through, in "concert style," the way she would play it for her teacher.

I moved my chair to the other side of the room, and suggested that before she begin to play, she decide just how she wanted the piece to sound. "You must attract my attention and interest with the very first note that you play," I said. She played the piece through, giving a delightful lilt to the sixteenth notes as they moved to the following chords. The Prelude now sounded like a charming little Spring song.

Just before she left, I summed up all that we had been doing, and said that the piece sounded ever so much better, and it certainly must feel more comfortable and be easier to play, now that we had studied it in such detail. I wrote in her notebook the things to remember when she practiced the Prelude at home:

1) Feel the count, "Three-*One*-Two," and the slackening on the second beat throughout the whole piece.

2) When you play the piece, *feel* with your fingertips the dotted eighth notes, and feel the gesture that your arm makes as each sixteenth note travels toward the following chord.

3) Make a beautiful splurge on the F♯ chord!

4) Be sure that you hear all those low bass notes and where they are moving.

We parted affectionately. Faith had been so interested and eager throughout that when she thanked me on leaving, I said, "I'm so glad you called me up, Faith. I can think of no pleasanter way of spending an hour than in bringing lovely music and a lovely person together. Your teacher will certainly have a beautiful surprise!"

GERTRUDE

BEETHOVEN SONATA — AWARENESS OF STRUCTURE — WAYS OF STUDYING

One of my most interesting interviews, though perhaps the most disheartening, was with Gertrude. She was an attractive girl, seventeen years old, and had studied the piano for ten years. She told me she had wanted to be a concert pianist, but had become so discouraged that she thought she'd give up music altogether. She came with her teacher, prepared to play the Beethoven F minor Sonata, Op. 2, No. 1.

I asked her how long she had been studying this sonata, and she replied, "About four or five months." At this point, her teacher interrupted from the other side of the room, "Why, Gertrude, you know you've been on it all year!"

Gertrude started playing. In spite of all the time she had spent on this piece, it was obvious that she had never come within "listening" distance of the meaning of the music. She was also baffled by many of the technical problems that the piece presented. She did not keep a steady speed, and when she came to the runs, she was playing almost twice as fast as when she started the movement. She was utterly "apart" from the sonata. She was making motions, and producing sounds that she did not hear. I wondered what motive could have kept her on the piano bench for ten years and on this piece for one, and thought what a pity it was that the piece itself had not had any fun for so long a time!

She played as far as the end of the Exposition, with the pedal held down several measures at a time. She was obviously very nervous, so I suggested that we stop and talk about the sonata.

A.D.:   Some of that is quite nice, Gertrude. But I think you don't really hear what you are playing. For one thing, you should use less pedal. Your ears really decide about your playing, and they tell your foot, as well as your fingers, what to do . . . Do you like this sonata?

Gertrude: Well, I am a little tired of it.

A.D.:   It really is a very exciting piece. We must find some things in it that you haven't heard. Now, let's see what we can discover about the first eight measures. Let's see what Beethoven is really talking about. What key is this piece in?

193

Gertrude: F minor.

A.D.: Right you are. He starts off with a broken F minor chord, and is headed first for the high A♭ and the turn around F. Will you play as far as that? It is marked *piano,* but we must all hear definitely that you are announcing the key of the piece.

(She played the first two measures.)

A.D.: As you know, that's the tonic triad. Have you ever studied any harmony, Gertrude?

Gertrude: Yes, one year.

A.D.: Did you recognize the chords that you were studying in the music you were playing?

Gertrude: No, we just wrote exercises.

A.D.: But you know, I'm sure, that after the tonic triad, the dominant chord is the most important in the key.

Gertrude: Yes, I remember that.

A.D.: Well, here Beethoven repeats the first figure, but now he uses the notes of the dominant seventh chord, going up to B♭, then curling around G. Won't you play it from the beginning, as far as that, and let us all hear that you are playing a repeated pattern.

(She played these four measures with much greater conviction than before.)

A.D.: That's good! Now, let me play what happens next.

(I illustrated on the piano as I talked.)

A.D.: He wants to reach the *fortissimo* F minor chord with the high C at the top. He seems impatient to get there, so, in order to have enough momentum to reach the C, he steps back, repeats the last measure of each of the two phrases with a *sforzando,* on A♭, one on B♭, and there he is, standing triumphantly on high C at the top! . . . You know, those climbers that finally reached the top of Mount Everest — the first thing they did was plant the Union Jack at the summit. Your high C must be "planted" just as definitely! (I continued playing.) Now he turns around, comes a little way down the slope, and rests quietly for a moment on the C major triad.

Everything that we have been talking about has been indicated by Beethoven. I'm glad you have the Urtext Edition, because all the markings are taken directly from Beethoven's manuscripts or from the first editions. Beethoven couldn't, of course, write everything that he meant, but he certainly meant everything that he did write! . . . Now, will you play those eight measures from the beginning?

(Gertrude did so. She was forgetting her nervousness, and was beginning to get interested in this kind of music study.)

A.D.:   Now, let's talk about the counting of this piece. What is the meter sign?

Gertrude: Alla breve. That means that you count two half notes in each measure.

A.D.:   Very true. But, you see, it begins on a quarter note, which does not come on any beat at all. So we have to decide how we're going to count it.

Gertrude (cheerfully): I always count it "And," because it's the "And" of "Two."

A.D.:   But where is the "Two"?

Gertrude: In the last measure of the piece, where it goes, "One-and-Two," and this C at the beginning of the piece is an incomplete measure.

A.D.:   It doesn't sound like that to me! I don't think that C at the beginning of the piece has anything at all to do with the last measure. As I hear it, that C is simply a short note that gives you a little impetus, starting you up the broken chord. In other words, it is a half beat *before* "One," but not a half beat *after* a "Two" that isn't there! The only question is what you're going to say in your counting. I've wondered so much about places like this. It is something like the word "The" at the beginning of a sentence. I've known a number of people in cases like this to say simply "Oo"! — which may sound silly, but certainly gets you started. "Oo-*One*." Try playing the first two measures, and count, "Oo - *One* - Two, *One* - Two."

(Gertrude tried playing the passage with this count, and found that it worked. She also discovered that the melodic phrase *ended* on "Two," so it probably did not *begin* on "Two.")

A.D.:   Of course, you could play the piece all the way through, counting "*One* - Two" in each measure. But it is more interesting musically, and certainly will be easier to play, if the measures are grouped in phrases, and if you count the number of beats in each *phrase*. First, let's see how long the phrases are. Surely, in order to make sense, the first two measures belong together, so the first phrase is two measures long. We can count the beats in the two measures, "Oo - *One* - Two - Three - Four."

Gertrude: Then I suppose you could count "*One*-Two-Three-Four" for the next two measures, too!

A.D.:   Yes, and how about the following measures?

Gertrude: The phrases seem shorter.

A.D.:   They are, and how are you going to count them?

(After a little trial and error, Gertrude decided that she could count "*One*-Two" twice over, followed by a last two-measure phrase, counted "*One* - Two - Three - Four.")

A.D.:   Now you have the rhythmic count of the whole passage. Counting the number of beats in each phrase this way gives you the Plan of the Count. Let me play the eight measures while you count the beats.

(We did so.)

Gertrude: It certainly sounds different!

A.D.:   It does, indeed! Now, *you* play it and count it this way, and be sure that you not only play with expression, but count with expression.

(She did this quite well, and the first eight measures of the sonata began to take form. I gave her a piece of paper and asked her to write the Plan of Count, putting a phrase on a line. She produced the following:

"Oo - *One* - Two - Three - Four,
           One - Two - Three - Four,
           One - Two,
           One - Two,
           One - Two - Three - Four.")

A.D.:   There are different ways of counting the same passage, but this will do to start you investigating. There *are* such things as strong measures and weak measures, just as there are strong beats and weak beats, and an even better way of counting this passage would perhaps be:

"Three - Four - *One* - Two,
 Three - Four - *One* - Two,
           One - Two,
           One - Two,
           One - Two - Three - Four."

(There was not time to make this detailed analysis of the whole of the Exposition, but I did want Gertrude to hear and understand two places: the suspensions leading to the second theme on E♭ [mm. 15-20], and the chords under the runs [mm. 33-41].)

A.D.:   Did you get as far as suspensions when you studied harmony?

Gertrude: Yes, we wrote some.

A.D.:   Did you ever play them?

Gertrude: No, it was a course in *written* harmony.

A.D.:   Well, there are some wonderful suspensions on this page. Beethoven is preparing to introduce his second theme. Let me play the beginning of the second theme for you.

(I played measures 21 through 25, to the G, and asked what key this passage was in. With help, she discovered that the key is A-flat — it *is* a difficult place for an untrained ear to hear.)

A.D.:   One of Beethoven's hallmarks is the dominant chord repeated over and over when he wants to make sure that you hear unmistakably the key that you are going to. Now, if you are heading for A-flat, what will be the dominant chord?

Gertrude (eventually): Eb.

A.D.:   Now listen to how Beethoven manages it.

(I played measures 15 through 20, calling her attention to the way the voices squeeze together three times toward Eb in the bass and G in the treble. In order to get her to hear the suspensions, I asked her to play this cadence very slowly without the suspensions: left hand Db D Eb, right hand Bb Ab G. Then she played the passage as written, and at once felt and heard the resistance of the suspended tones in the right hand, as they are dragged downward to their resolution. Gradually she understood the meaning of the music, as Beethoven exerts more and more energy and contrary motion to bring the hands together on the dominant chord. She played the five measures and asked: "Is that what you want?")

A.D.:   Not especially! What I want is to help you to find out what you think Beethoven wants, and to help you to do it.

(Then I asked her to play the descending scale passages at the end of the Exposition, starting with measure 33. They were fast and superficial, as though she were doing a technical exercise.)

A.D.:   Gertrude, you sound to me as though you were sliding down the banisters! Scales almost always have chords implied underneath them. Even a scale that is played by a violin alone, or sung by a singer, has almost always a chord background. A scale isn't a glorified finger exercise. It is a sort of decoration of the underlying harmony.

Gertrude: What do you mean?

A.D.:   Well, play the scale of C slowly up one octave.

Gertrude: At least I can do that!

A.D.:   Scales sometimes seem to me like chords laid sideways with
           notes in between. For instance, the scale that you played
           sounds like C E G and high C, decorated with passing notes.
           Won't you play first the broken chord, and then the scale,
           and you'll hear what I mean.

Gertrude: Yes, I can hear that. But what has it to do with the
           Beethoven scales?

A.D.:   The idea is the same: Beethoven's scale starts off, supported
           in the left hand by a broken chord, C Eb Ab. In the next
           measure the scale continues coming down, but now it is
           supported by the chord Db F Bb. Then you play decorations
           around Eb, first with Eb Ab C in the bass, and then
           Db Bb G Eb. So, you see, the scale is changing its harmonic
           meaning twice, and the Eb also has two meanings.

           Actually, it seems to me that the left hand is much more
           important here than the right hand. Play the left hand alone,
           and notice the pattern. The same idea is repeated three times,
           and Beethoven makes this clear by writing *sforzando* in the
           same place in each of the three measures. This bass line is a
           fine syncopated melody in its own right.

(Gertrude played the left-hand part with much more understanding
than before.)

A.D.:   Here is another way of exploring this passage. Try playing
           both hands together, but this time play the left-hand notes
           of each measure in solid chords. Play only one measure at a
           time, stopping on the last note in the right hand, until you
           have heard which notes of the scale are duplicating the notes
           of the chord.

(Gertrude did this easily, too.)

A.D.:   Now play the passage as it really is. You have a fine 'cello
           melody in your left hand, and in your right, a beautiful
           decorating scale with all the violins. Beethoven was, of course,
           an orchestral composer, and a great deal of his piano music
           sounds as though it might have been written for the or-
           chestra . . . Well, Gertrude, I think we've made a good start
           exploring the Exposition of this sonata, don't you?

Gertrude: The what of the sonata?

A.D.:   The Exposition. Have you ever heard of Sonata Form?

Gertrude: (although she had already played three Beethoven sonatas!)
           No. We only did Harmony.

(So I explained in the simplest terms:)

A.D.:   The first movement of a sonata is usually written in what is called "Sonata Form." It is something like a play in three acts. There are two main characters, like the hero and the heroine of a play. They are called the First Theme and the Second Theme. In this sonata, Act I starts with the hero coming on stage — that is the F minor theme at the very beginning. Then there is a Bridge leading to where the lady comes in — the lyrical theme in A-flat major. This is Part One, and is called the Statement, or the Exposition. Will you write the word "Statement" in your music at the beginning of the movement? . . . The Statement ends at the double bar, and now comes Act II, called the Development. Will you write "Development" after the double bar. Here the themes have all kinds of adventures. The plot thickens! In your sonata, the Development section is quite short. At the end there is a wonderful passage leading to Act III. This act is the culmination of the story, and is called the Restatement, or sometimes, the Recapitulation. Can you find in the music the place where the Restatement begins? The melody is the same as at the beginning of the piece, but now, instead of being quiet, it sounds stormy and angry.

Gertrude: Is it on this page?

A.D.:   I'm asking you — not telling you! I want you to discover it yourself!

(With a little help she found and marked the Restatement.)

A.D.:   Here again is Theme One, still in F minor. When the heroine, Theme Two, comes back, she says to the hero, "I shall continue my own theme, but I will do it in your key — in F minor." Many classic sonatas are written in this form. Why don't you write this down in your notebook? (And I dictated the following:—)

Outline of Sonata Form

Statement—Theme I and Theme 2 in different but related keys.

Development—The same material in many keys.

Restatement—Both themes in the first key.

A.D.:   In reading or seeing a play, it's more interesting if you know the cast of characters, isn't it?

Gertrude: Of course.

A.D.:   Well, I think you'll enjoy playing this sonata more, now that you know its characters.

Gertrude: I used to play a Haydn sonata. Are his sonatas like this?

A.D.:   I'm glad you brought that up. Haydn really started developing this form. When you come to Beethoven, it's more closely knit. Incidentally, did you know that Mozart started the last movement of his G minor Symphony with practically the same idea that Beethoven used in beginning this F minor Sonata that you play? (I played the two passages in succession.) The first seven notes are exactly the same. But then Beethoven repeats his phrase and drives home his point. Mozart does something quite different. He writes a contrasting phrase.

Gertrude: Which is the best?

A.D.:   You can't compare them that way. They are just instances of how two composers worked out the same idea.

Gertrude: But Mozart must have copied it from Beethoven!

A.D.:   No, I'm afraid it would have been the other way round. Mozart died before this sonata was published. But no one really copies anyone, except deliberately, perhaps, for a musical joke. There are literally thousands of themes that could be made out of a broken chord like this one. You could make up a melody yourself, beginning with that minor chord.

          But as far as your Beethoven sonata is concerned, Gertrude, there is much more in the piece than you were getting out. In music like this, you know, there is no end to what you can discover! I've known this piece for fifty years, and yet, today, I heard some things in it that I never noticed before!

Gertrude: I know I didn't play it very well for you. But I always misinterpret, anyway!

A.D. (astonished): You're an intelligent girl, Gertrude, but that's a most *un*intelligent remark! Music is not a possession, it's a trust. It's up to you to find out what's in the music. Interpretation isn't something you add on to the music after you've learned the notes. The music is there, and it's your business to see behind those printed notes and rests and marks of expression, what the music means, and how it must sound. It's an obligation you owe to the music, and to Beethoven, to find out what he means, and to bring it to life in sound. You learn that by study, as we have been doing now, not by practicing the notes over and over.

You have good fast fingers. You know, the great Polish pianist Paderewski had his hands insured by Lloyd's of London for almost a million dollars, as I remember. I was talking to another pianist, Harold Bauer, one day, and asked him if he, too, had his hands insured. He replied, "No, my hands are not insured. That would be useless. Because the first thing I would have to insure is my head, and I doubt that they sell that kind of insurance!"

Gertrude, if I were you, I would give this sonata a little rest. Then, before you begin to practice it again, I would sit in a comfortable chair with the music. Look over the sonata as far as we have studied it. Try to remember the things we have discovered and talked about today, and try to hear inside your head the way you want the music to sound. Then go to the piano and play it, and see if it doesn't sound more sensible and more beautiful. Study the whole sonata this way . . . Well, the sermon is over! . . . Oh, before you go, do play the wonderful ending of the movement.

(Gertrude played the last seven measures.)

Gertrude: I never can get them loud enough.

A.D.: You are right — they are loud. It is very surprising. Just when the movement seems to be ending quietly, Beethoven bursts forth with these impatient *fortissimo* chords.

(As she rose to go, I said, "Well, Gertrude, you and Beethoven and I have had an interesting session. Isn't it an exciting piece?")

Gertrude: It certainly is different from what I thought. I do understand it better.

(We shook hands, and Gertrude left the room.)

Her teacher came forward and said, "Thank you so much, Miss Diller. I did enjoy seeing how you teach. I approve of your approach. But in my lessons, I don't have time to take up this side of music."

To which I could only reply, "But, my dear Mrs. J., it is not a matter of this side or that side. All that concerns us about music is the inside."

MARY

Playing Legato — Weight Touch — Using the Pedal — "O God, Our Help in Ages Past"

Mary was a middle-aged colored woman who was housekeeper for a friend whom I was visiting. She was a most unusual person — very calm, very intelligent, and most kind. She did everything in the house: looked after us all, cooked delicious meals, drove the car, and was a delightfully unhurried member of the household. She loved music. She sang soprano in the choir of the church she attended, and had always wished that she could play the piano.

She had had two unfortunate experiences with piano lessons. Her first teacher had started her off on a book of "61 Favorite Piano Pieces." These, she thought, were beautiful, but since even the easiest was far too difficult for her, she said, "I got completely discouraged." A second teacher reduced her to boredom with a diet consisting exclusively of scales and exercises. After that, Mary decided to "give up" the piano. But during my visit we became friends and she said she would like to try *my* "method."

Mary had only fifteen minutes a day to practice, and sometimes not that, but she was so eager to learn that she progressed very quickly in her music study. During the month of my visit, we had five sessions together at the piano, and Mary learned to read some easy folk tunes and a "piece," and learned to play some chords, and learned a rote piece, and how to use the pedal. She was charmed with these new experiences, and was most responsive. Her frequent remark was "I see what you mean!"

Mary touched the keys gently and lovingly, but her way of playing had been to drop the wrist after every note, so that all the tones were disconnected. She did not know how to play legato, so our first task was to develop the so-called "weight touch."

Mary found that if she held her arm slightly raised, the weight of hand and arm would center on her fingertips. She soon got the sensation of balancing the weight on each fingertip in turn, and shifting smoothly from one finger to another. "It's like crossing a brook on stepping stones," I said. "You poise and get your balance where you are before you move on to the next stone."

Her ear was good, and she heard with pleasure the tone qualities

she was making with her new "weight touch." She experimented first
with a five-finger exercise, and then with a melodic phrase. Since the
tones of a melody are connected from the first note to the last, she found
that she could easily play legato by shifting the weight from one fingertip to the next, letting her upper arm travel always in the direction of
the melody.

The great excitement, however, was learning to use the damper
pedal. First we inspected the interior of the piano, and she discovered
the action of the dampers on the strings.

Then she found that if she kept her foot on the pedal, she could
play the notes of a chord in several octaves, and that it would sound
beautiful. We made up the following exercise:

First she pressed the damper pedal down, and then she played in
the right hand, C E G, singing the letter names as she played. Still
holding the pedal down, she played the notes of the same chord in
open position in this succession: beginning in a lower octave, left hand
C G, right hand above E C, left hand crossing over to the C one octave
higher. This is what she played:

She listened to the tones she had produced, and said with a beaming
smile, "It sounds so professional — and so soon!"

She experimented with many single chords, following the same pattern, and enjoyed the sound as she heard each chord-mass that she
was producing.

Next she learned how to operate the pedal if she were going to play
changing chords. First she practiced the movement of the foot alone,
moving the pedal up and down, and "talking" to her foot, saying aloud
"up-down, up-down" as she did so. She realized that in order to avoid
blurring, she must make this "up-down" motion every time she played
a new harmony.

This pedal technique she put into immediate use the following morning.

I heard Mary working in the kitchen, and, going in, found her busy with the breakfast dishes. I asked her if sometime she would like to learn how to play a hymn tune on the piano. Removing her hands from the dishpan, she said, "Can't we do it now? I can wash the dishes any time!"

So we went to the piano. I got out a hymn book, and turned to "O God, Our Help in Ages Past." Mary knew this melody, and was eager to learn to play the hymn.

It was written in C major, with two notes of each chord in the right hand, and two in the left throughout, with only a few exceptions. The time-values were entirely uncomplicated, so they presented no problem.

Before starting to play, we looked over the music. She learned that the tune was in 4 meter, and that the count was "Four/*One* Two Three," that there were four phrases each two measures long, and that each phrase ended on count "Three." Then she began studying the first phrase in detail. Here are the first four chords of the first phrase:

Now she started learning to play these chords. Looking at the right-hand part alone, she named the notes she was going to play. I asked her to tell me what she discovered about them, and she said, "Your thumb plays C four times — I suppose the Alto sings that. The Soprano begins on G, then goes to E, then it jumps to A, and then goes back again to G, where it started." Now she practiced the right-hand part alone until she felt secure. She balanced on each pair of notes until her fingers were ready to play the next pair, and she changed the pedal on each chord.

Then she studied the left-hand part, and said, "The Bass plays C twice, and the Tenor goes from E up to G. Why, that's just the opposite of what the Soprano did when she went from G to E! Then you play F alone — I suppose both the Tenor and the Bass are singing it. Then the Bass goes down from F to E, and the Tenor goes up from F to G." She played these left-hand chords several times, and then played the four chords with both hands together.

Using the same technique of looking ahead and describing the finger moves, she learned the rest of the phrase.

"Can you finish learning this hymn by yourself?" I asked. Mary said that she was sure that she could. I told her that I was more interested in showing her how to study any hymn tunes she might want to learn, than in teaching her how to play this one particular tune. So I asked her to make notes in her assignment book of the following list of "Reminders," which I dictated to her. This is what she wrote:

On Learning to Play Hymn Tunes

1. Think of a hymn tune as built of voices moving horizontally from left to right across the page, and not as a succession of vertical chords.
2. Go slow, and study only a phrase at a time, and repeat it until you feel comfortable and confident that it is under your fingers.
3. Practice each phrase hands separately, then play hands together.
4. Keep the weight of your arm on your fingertips as you play each chord.
5. When you move from one chord to the next, always look ahead, and find the *easy* things. See if a note is repeated, and notice which way and how far the other notes move. When you have decided this, shift the weight to the fingertips of the next chord.
6. Change the pedal "Up-down" for each chord.

Mary went back into the kitchen. She resumed washing the dishes, but was now lightening her toil by singing gently and happily, "O God, Our Help in Ages Past."

On the last day of my visit at the end of the month, Mary played a "program" for my friend. It consisted of all the major triads played as broken chords in two hands, *with* the pedal; playing half a dozen little folk-tune melodies involving a variety of touches (legato, staccato, diminuendo, and crescendo); playing a one-page piece entirely on black keys, "Swans in the Moonlight," which she had learned by rote. Then, as a test in sight reading, she played the right-hand part of the "Blue Danube" Waltz, and ended up with "O God, Our Help in Ages Past" — which she had finished learning by herself!

Mary's joy at being able to play these pieces and do such a variety of things at the piano was very moving. My friend complimented her, and Mary said, "I never knew that you could study music and talk about it! I never knew about phrasing. I never knew about the pedal before. I couldn't read at all — I just picked out the notes one at a time and tried to play them. But now I see you read music right along the line, the way you read a book . . . It's marvelous . . . It's really thrilling!"

Mary's pleasure was matched by my own, for I considered it a privilege to have been able to open out a new world to this eager, sensitive soul.

MISS ROBERTS

Bach's "Italian Concerto" — Last Movement of the "Moonlight" Sonata — Counting the Chopin C major Prelude

Miss Roberts was a teacher of wide experience who had been teaching for many years and had a large class of devoted pupils. She attended a course in musical pedagogy that I was conducting in a California college town, and in addition, had some individual piano lessons with me.

She had studied with a variety of teachers. For two years before we met, she had been taking lessons from a well-known pianist who put all of his pupils through the same technical mill. She had practiced a large repertory of pieces, but everything, from Mozart to Debussy, was first approached as a finger exercise. Every piece was first played in whole notes *fortissimo*. While she was building up this technique, musical content and interpretation were never mentioned in the lessons. Occasionally she would ask her teacher about the phrasing of a certain passage, and his invariable reply was, "Don't bother about that now. You must first master the technique." Miss Roberts was a most conscientious person, and had had an almost puritanical feeling that this technical regimen, once begun, had to be endured to the end. She told me that after two years of these lessons, he made the astonishing statement: "You have perfected your technique, Miss Roberts. We will now study as music the pieces that you have been practicing."

At this point she discontinued the lessons.

Several months later, when we were working together, she called upon her former teacher and told him that she was studying with me. She reported that, over a cup of tea, his only comment was, "I hope she hasn't spoiled your technique."

When she first came to me, she played everything from Bach to Chopin with a uniformly sharp and brittle tone, and well-articulated finger action. She had great fleetness and much strength, but was so concerned with the mechanics of doing certain things with her fingers and hands that she did not really hear the sounds that she was producing.

At one of her early lessons with me, we began studying the Bach "Italian" Concerto, which had been in her repertory for some time. She played the first movement, and it sounded very dry. There was no rhythmic "give" to her performance, because all the notes were played

207

with metronomic evenness, and the tones were detached as though she were speaking not words but hyphenated syllables.

We started analyzing the first eight measures. Bach begins, characteristically, by "setting up" the tonality of the piece. He announces the tonic triad in the first four measures, and the dominant triad in the next four. He begins with an "explosion" of the F major triad in the left hand, then the right hand continues building up the F major harmony. To my ear, the third and fifth of the chord, A and C, which occur together three times in the first four measures, are each time the objective of a rhythmic impulse: first as the end of a rising figure, then as the end of a two-note descending figure, and finally as the end of a melodic curve, ending with a suspension. This grouping is indicated in the following illustration:

In order to play this passage in a way that would bring out the harmonic meaning, I suggested that, in the right hand part, she make the slightest pause on A and C — the terminal notes of the little figures, until her ear had registered the F major harmony each time, and her fingers were aware of the keys they were touching.

Having established the F major chord, Bach now proceeds to the dominant, and repeats the passage in sequence on the harmony of C major.

Miss Roberts had studied written harmony and had analyzed much music, but her study had largely been confined to identifying chords with figures. The chords in many of her pieces were marked with figured bass notation. She had not really heard the movement between the chords, or realized their meaning, so she was intrigued by the kind of harmonic analysis we applied to the first eight measures of the concerto. In the first four measures, the chord scheme is I, IV to I, IV to I with a suspension. In the next four measures, it is V, I to V, I to V with a suspension. She was interested to find that the movement of the harmonies was the clue to the phrasing.

We worked through the rest of the movement in similar fashion.

She was growing more and more excited, as she began to hear the sense of the music that she had played mechanically for so long. She had been in the habit of playing all metrical groups of four sixteenth notes as though they belonged together rhythmically:

She found that in many passages of this first movement, the patterns of sixteenth notes grouped

"sounded better and were easier to play," as she put it. Here again, she found that if she made the *slightest* pause on the last note of each little group, the phrasing became clear and intelligible.

The first movement took shape and hung together as she began to realize the interrelationship of many of the parts.

We spoke of the relative speed of the first and third movements, serving as a frame for the quiet lyricism of the Andante. She had thought of the first and third movements as being played at the same speed. But on consideration, she realized that the brilliant finale was the quicker of the two, and that the first movement should be played at a slower tempo than she had been taking it. I have always felt that the first movement should be played with a certain deliberation. It has something of the fanfare quality of an overture.

We worked on the slow movement, studying the interplay of the three horizontal strands of music: the reiterated pattern of thirds in the center of the mass, resting on the repeated pairs of bass notes, and all as undercurrent to the flowing floriated melodic line. Miss Roberts had played the organ, and realized that this movement has the timbre of organ music, with the right hand playing the melody, the left hand playing the continuing accompaniment in thirds, while the low bass notes would be played on the pedal. Miss Roberts was fascinated to analyze the contemplative harmonic opening of this movement, where Bach sets up the harmonic scheme in D minor with the chords I, IV, V_7 I, a chord for each measure over a low D pedal point.

Her facile technique made the playing of the last movement easy, once she heard what the music was doing. Altogether, she found that the study of this composition was an ear-opener and mind-opener of great value.

She was a most eager-minded student, once she was released from a purely technical approach and encouraged to explore the music she was studying. She had been so bound by her absorption in technical facts that she was greatly excited to be dealing with musical ideas. One of the ideas we discussed was that one must often search for the appropriate technical gesture that will best bring out the musical meaning of a particular passage. This was a new idea to Miss Roberts. She had thought of technique as being a skill uniformly applied to all pieces alike. She was surprised to discover that technique can be varied and entertaining.

At one lesson, Miss Roberts played the last movement of the Beethoven "Moonlight" Sonata. She held her forearm level throughout, and relied solely on finger action. It sounded like a glorified Czerny exercise.

We analyzed together the gestures that would make it easy to bring out the melodic contours that are inherent in the music. We started with the right-hand passage at the beginning of the movement. Here a series of rising broken chords mounts with growing excitement to the final eruption of the chord at the top and its immediate echo. She found that if she played each broken chord with an outward rotary motion of the upper arm, she could make a series of crescendos, because the weight would be tilted away from the thumb and toward the little finger. This gesture would bring out the contour and the emotional meaning of the passage convincingly. I suggested that she practice the gesture of playing the two culminating chords at the top of each passage, first on the lid of the piano, playing the second echoing chord like the rebound of a bouncing ball. This gesture was easily transferred to the keyboard.

In the left hand, in order to bring out the reiterated C♯, she rotated the upper arm from the thumb toward the little finger, making the movement from G♯ to C♯. This brought a comfortable feeling when the hands were played together, since the rotating of both arms outward tilted the weight toward the two fifth fingers simultaneously.

She worked out the gestures for the rest of the movement by herself, and was delighted to find that she was becoming more and more an independent student of technique as well as of music.

Her curiosity was growing by leaps and bounds. Often when she came to a lesson, my first remark would be, "What have you been finding out this week?" and she would eagerly recount the many astonishing discoveries she had made, not only in the music she was studying, but also in the music she was teaching.

She was a most enthusiastic teacher, and her relations with her pupils were unusually warm and friendly. She took them in groups to concerts and the opera, and had many ingenious ways of keeping alive their interest in music. During the months that we worked together, we went over much of the music that she was teaching, and she would always begin by giving me a delightful word picture of the pupil who was going to study the piece we were discussing.

One day she told me of a teen-age boy who was working on the Chopin C major Prelude, Op. 28, No. 1. She said, "He is having a dreadful time with it! It sounds so lumpy, and I don't know how to help him." I asked her how he counted the piece, and she replied, "He counts *One*-Two for every measure." My first reaction was that this was probably the reason why it sounded so lumpy! And I suggested that if he counted in groups of *measures* — that is, in phrase lengths rather than in beats — the Prelude would sound more flowing.

The meter is $\frac{2}{8}$, and the beats come so quickly that if every beat is counted, it sounds like a fast and rather jumpy piece, which it is not. But if the piece is thought of with one count to each measure, considering each measure as a beat, the effect will be much slower, even though the notes are played at the same speed. The underlying principle, of course, is that the impression of fastness or slowness that we have in listening to music is given by the speed of the *beats,* and not by the speed of the *notes*.

We also discussed the fact that in music there are weak measures and strong measures, just as there are weak beats and strong beats. The rhythmic meaning of this piece is lucidly expressed if we recognize that the count of measures begins with a pattern of "Three Four *One* Two."

We wrote out the Plan of Count of the entire piece as follows, with each count representing one measure, and putting a phrase on a line, as poetry would be written.

Three Four | *One* Two,
Three Four | *One* Two,
Three Four | *One* Two,
Three Four | *One* Two,
Three Four Five Six | *One* Two Three Four | *One*
Two | *One*

Two | *One* Two Three Four | *One* Two.

She reported at a later lesson that the boy was able to play the Prelude with fluency after he had counted groups of measures in this way, and so had heard the piece in its natural phrase lengths.

Miss Roberts was a most stimulating student. I was delighted to hear recently that she was planning to start a school of her own, where I am sure the pupils will learn music, as well as piano playing.

Part VIII.

RECAPITULATION

This book concludes with a brief summary of the subject matter that we have been discussing.

In Part I we spoke first of the function of the Interpreter, and emphasized his responsibility. We spoke of the diversity of possible interpretations of the same composition, and said that a fine performance may reveal beauties that perhaps were unknown even to the composer himself.

Since Performers have to be taught, Part II deals with Teachers, their own preparation to teach music, and their great opportunity for releasing music in their students. Class teaching and individual lessons are discussed. There is a brief survey of some of the changes that have taken place in piano teaching during the last fifty years.

Part III, "Teaching Accompanied by Learning," consists of several chapters on subject matter that is part of the music lesson, including Phrasing, Counting, Ear Training, and Piano Technique.

Part IV describes ways of humanizing Pupils' Recitals and the Spring Concert.

Part V has to do with the relationship between Parents and Teachers, and Parents and Children.

Part VI contains suggestions for dealing with the Adult Beginner, and the student who comes from another teacher.

Part VII, "Listening In," comprises a number of "case histories" — accounts of lessons given to a variety of students of all ages, from a five-year-old to a mature and experienced teacher.

CODA

Before the final cadence, I should like to make a comparison between Arts that are expressed in Space — architecture, sculpture, and painting — and the Art of Music, which is expressed in Time.

By the very nature of their materials, Arts that are expressed in Space are subject to deterioration and the ravages of Time. The Arts of Space are perhaps at their highest point of perfection at the moment when they are finished by their creators. But, with the passage of the years, the Parthenon crumbles, Rheims Cathedral may be bombed, the Venus de Milo loses her arms, the Winged Victory loses her head, and the "Night Watch" may be slashed by a vandal.

Great music, however, cannot deteriorate. Music that is dull or cheap has not sufficient inner vitality to survive over the years. But great music endures in its own right. It is born anew whenever it is heard.

Music, when it is performed, unfolds sequentially, and there is a necessary passage of time between the first note of a composition and the last. Although while it is being performed it is fleeting and evanescent, music in reality is durable and indestructible.

Music, whose re-creation is expressed in Time, is timeless.

214